EVEN IF

a study of Habakkuk

KRISTIN SCHMUCKER

Study Suggestions

We believe that the Bible is true, trustworthy, and timeless and that it is vitally important for all believers. These study suggestions are intended to help you more effectively study Scripture as you seek to know and love God through His Word.

SUGGESTED STUDY TOOLS

- A Bible

- A double-spaced, printed copy of the Scripture passages that this study covers. You can use a website like *www.biblegateway.com* to copy the text of a passage and print out a double-spaced copy to be able to mark on easily

- A journal to write notes or prayers

- Pens, colored pencils, and highlighters

- A dictionary to look up unfamiliar words

HOW TO USE THIS STUDY

Begin your study time in prayer. Ask God to reveal Himself to you, to help you understand what you are reading, and to transform you with His Word (Psalm 119:18).

Before you read what is written in each day of the study itself, read the assigned passages of Scripture for that day. Use your double-spaced copy to circle, underline, highlight, draw arrows, and mark in any way you would like to help you dig deeper as you work through a passage.

Read the daily written content provided for the current study day.

Answer the questions that appear at the end of each study day.

HOW TO STUDY THE BIBLE

The inductive method provides tools for deeper and more intentional Bible study. To study the Bible inductively, work through the steps below after reading background information on the book.

1. OBSERVATION & COMPREHENSION
Key question: What does the text say?

After reading the daily Scripture in its entirety at least once, begin working with smaller portions of the Scripture. Read a passage of Scripture repetitively, and then mark the following items in the text:

- Key or repeated words and ideas
- Key themes
- Transition words (Ex: therefore, but, because, if/then, likewise, etc.)
- Lists
- Comparisons and contrasts
- Commands
- Unfamiliar words (look these up in a dictionary)
- Questions you have about the text

2. INTERPRETATION
Key question: What does the text mean?

Once you have annotated the text, work through the following steps to help you interpret its meaning:

- Read the passage in other versions for a better understanding of the text.
- Read cross-references to help interpret Scripture with Scripture.
- Paraphrase or summarize the passage to check for understanding.
- Identify how the text reflects the metanarrative of Scripture, which is the story of creation, fall, redemption, and restoration.
- Read trustworthy commentaries if you need further insight into the meaning of the passage.

3 APPLICATION

Key Question: How should the truth of this passage change me?

Bible study is not merely an intellectual pursuit. The truths about God, ourselves, and the gospel that we discover in Scripture should produce transformation in our hearts and lives. Answer the following questions as you consider what you have learned in your study:

- What attributes of God's character are revealed in the passage?

    Consider places where the text directly states the character of God, as well as how His character is revealed through His words and actions.

- What do I learn about myself in light of who God is?

    Consider how you fall short of God's character, how the text reveals your sin nature, and what it says about your new identity in Christ.

- How should this truth change me?

    A passage of Scripture may contain direct commands telling us what to do or warnings about sins to avoid in order to help us grow in holiness. Other times our application flows out of seeing ourselves in light of God's character. As we pray and reflect on how God is calling us to change in light of His Word, we should be asking questions like, "How should I pray for God to change my heart?" and "What practical steps can I take toward cultivating habits of holiness?"

THE ATTRIBUTES OF GOD

ETERNAL
God has no beginning and no end. He always was, always is, and always will be.

HAB. 1:12 / REV. 1:8 / IS. 41:4

FAITHFUL
God is incapable of anything but fidelity. He is loyally devoted to His plan and purpose.

2 TIM. 2:13 / DEUT. 7:9
HEB. 10:23

GOOD
God is pure; there is no defilement in Him. He is unable to sin, and all He does is good.

GEN. 1:31 / PS. 34:8 / PS. 107:1

GRACIOUS
God is kind, giving us gifts and benefits we do not deserve.

2 KINGS 13:23 / PS. 145:8
IS. 30:18

HOLY
God is undefiled and unable to be in the presence of defilement. He is sacred and set-apart.

REV. 4:8 / LEV. 19:2 / HAB. 1:13

INCOMPREHENSIBLE & TRANSCENDENT
God is high above and beyond human understanding. He is unable to be fully known.

PS. 145:3 / IS. 55:8-9
ROM. 11:33-36

IMMUTABLE
God does not change. He is the same yesterday, today, and tomorrow.

1 SAM. 15:29 / ROM. 11:29
JAMES 1:17

INFINITE
God is limitless. He exhibits all of His attributes perfectly and boundlessly.

ROM. 11:33-36 / IS. 40:28
PS. 147:5

JEALOUS
God is desirous of receiving the praise and affection He rightly deserves.

EX. 20:5 / DEUT. 4:23-24
JOSH. 24:19

JUST
God governs in perfect justice. He acts in accordance with justice. In Him, there is no wrongdoing or dishonesty.

IS. 61:8 / DEUT. 32:4 / PS. 146:7-9

LOVING
God is eternally, enduringly, steadfastly loving and affectionate. He does not forsake or betray His covenant love.

JN. 3:16 / EPH. 2:4-5 / 1 JN. 4:16

MERCIFUL

God is compassionate, withholding from us the wrath that we deserve.

TITUS 3:5 / PS. 25:10
LAM. 3:22-23

OMNIPOTENT

God is all-powerful; His strength is unlimited.

MAT. 19:26 / JOB 42:1-2
JER. 32:27

OMNIPRESENT

God is everywhere; His presence is near and permeating.

PROV. 15:3 / PS. 139:7-10
JER. 23:23-24

OMNISCIENT

God is all-knowing; there is nothing unknown to Him.

PS. 147:4 / I JN. 3:20
HEB. 4:13

PATIENT

God is long-suffering and enduring. He gives ample opportunity for people to turn toward Him.

ROM. 2:4 / 2 PET. 3:9 / PS. 86:15

SELF-EXISTENT

God was not created but exists by His power alone.

PS. 90:1-2 / JN. 1:4 / JN. 5:26

SELF-SUFFICIENT

God has no needs and depends on nothing, but everything depends on God.

IS. 40:28-31 / ACTS 17:24-25
PHIL. 4:19

SOVEREIGN

God governs over all things; He is in complete control.

COL. 1:17 / PS. 24:1-2
1 CHRON. 29:11-12

TRUTHFUL

God is our measurement of what is fact. By Him we are able to discern true and false.

JN. 3:33 / ROM. 1:25 / JN. 14:6

WISE

God is infinitely knowledgeable and is judicious with His knowledge.

IS. 46:9-10 / IS. 55:9 / PROV. 3:19

WRATHFUL

God stands in opposition to all that is evil. He enacts judgment according to His holiness, righteousness, and justice.

PS. 69:24 / JN. 3:36 / ROM. 1:18

Study Suggestions

TIMELINE OF SCRIPTURE

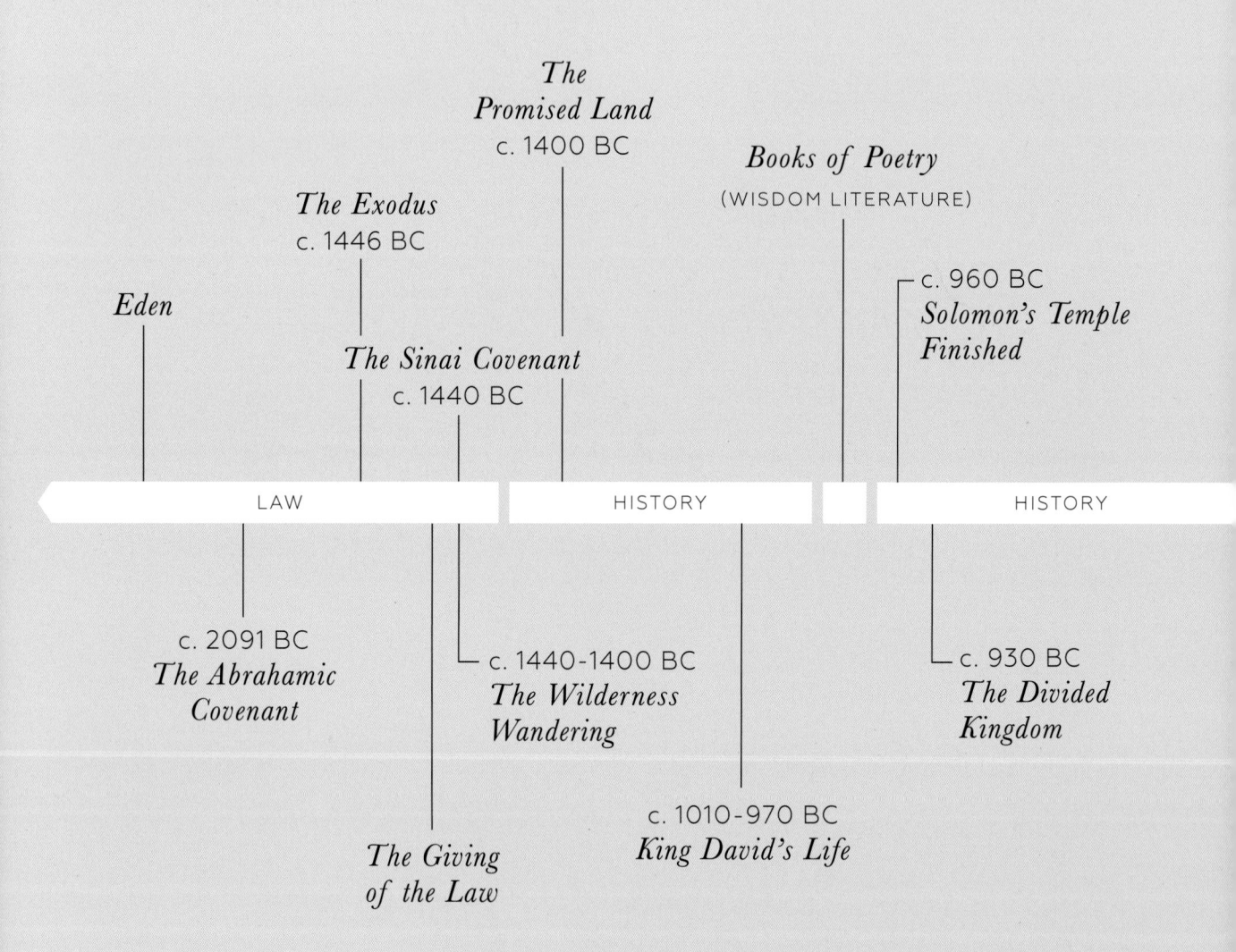

Eden

The Exodus
c. 1446 BC

The Sinai Covenant
c. 1440 BC

The Promised Land
c. 1400 BC

Books of Poetry
(WISDOM LITERATURE)

c. 960 BC
Solomon's Temple Finished

LAW — **HISTORY** — **HISTORY**

c. 2091 BC
The Abrahamic Covenant

c. 1440-1400 BC
The Wilderness Wandering

The Giving of the Law

c. 1010-970 BC
King David's Life

c. 930 BC
The Divided Kingdom

- c. 722 BC
Israel Exiled to Assyria

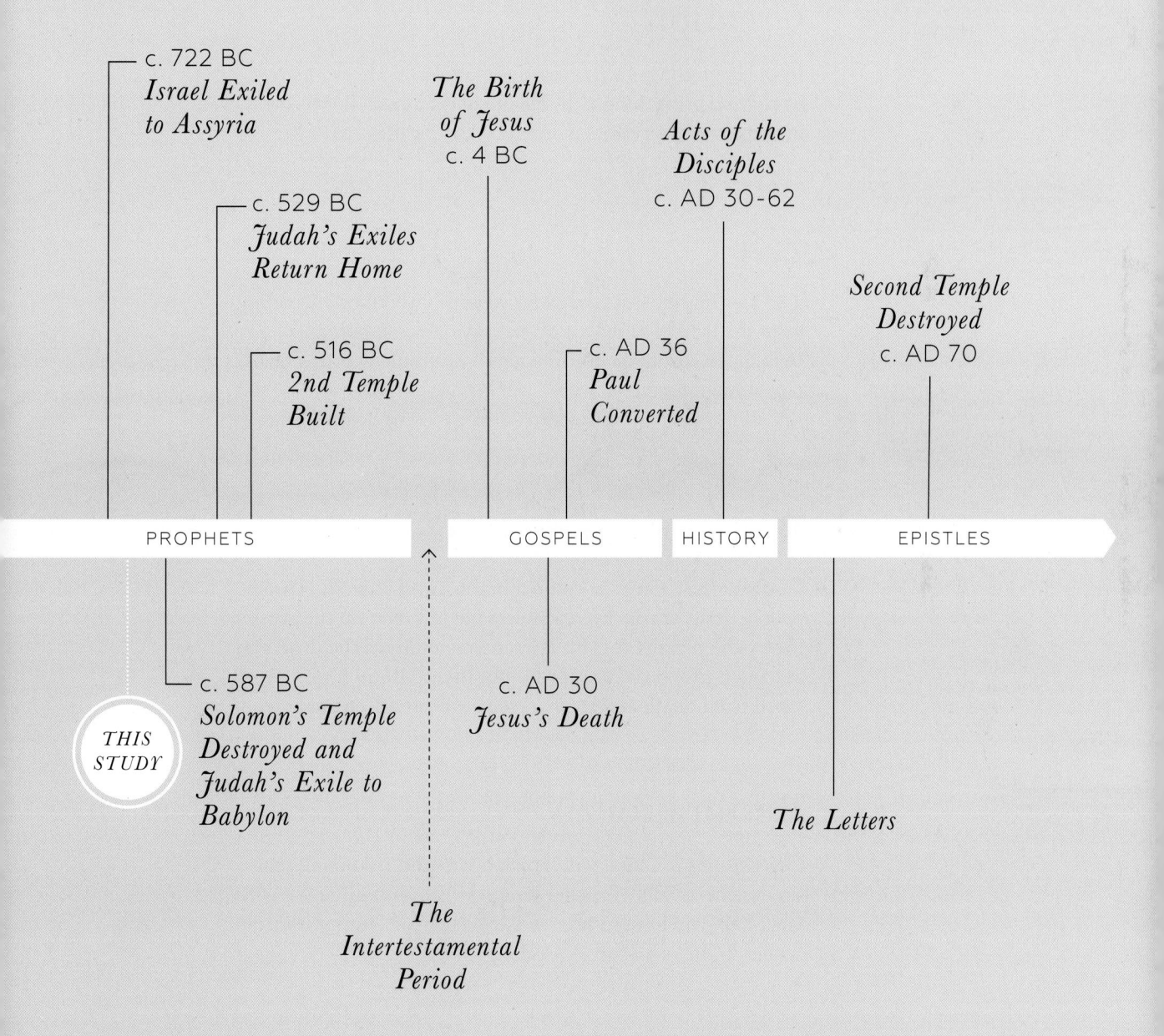

- c. 529 BC
Judah's Exiles Return Home

- c. 516 BC
2nd Temple Built

The Birth of Jesus
c. 4 BC

Acts of the Disciples
c. AD 30-62

Second Temple Destroyed
c. AD 70

- c. AD 36
Paul Converted

PROPHETS — GOSPELS — HISTORY — EPISTLES

THIS STUDY

- c. 587 BC
Solomon's Temple Destroyed and Judah's Exile to Babylon

c. AD 30
Jesus's Death

The Letters

The Intertestamental Period

Study Suggestions / 9

METANARRATIVE OF SCRIPTURE

Creation

In the beginning, God created the universe. He made the world and everything in it. He created humans in His own image to be His representatives on the earth.

Fall

The first humans, Adam and Eve, disobeyed God by eating from the fruit of the Tree of Knowledge of Good and Evil. Their disobedience impacted the whole world. The punishment for sin is death, and because of Adam's original sin, all humans are sinful and condemned to death.

Redemption

God sent His Son to become a human and redeem His people. Jesus Christ lived a sinless life but died on the cross to pay the penalty for sin. He resurrected from the dead and ascended into heaven. All who put their faith in Jesus are saved from death and freely receive the gift of eternal life.

Restoration

One day, Jesus Christ will return again and restore all that sin destroyed. He will usher in a new heaven and new earth where all who trust in Him will live eternally with glorified bodies in the presence of God.

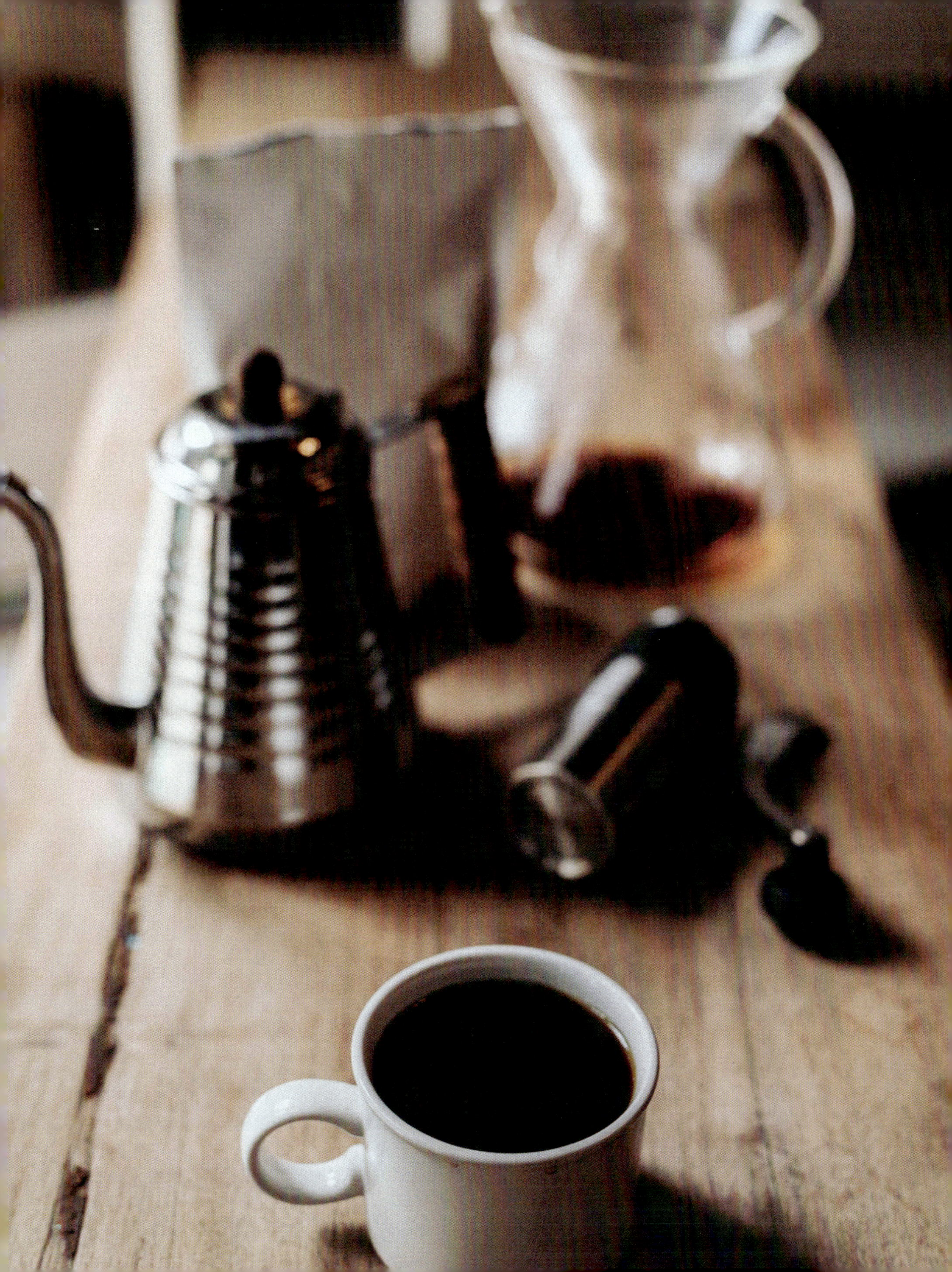

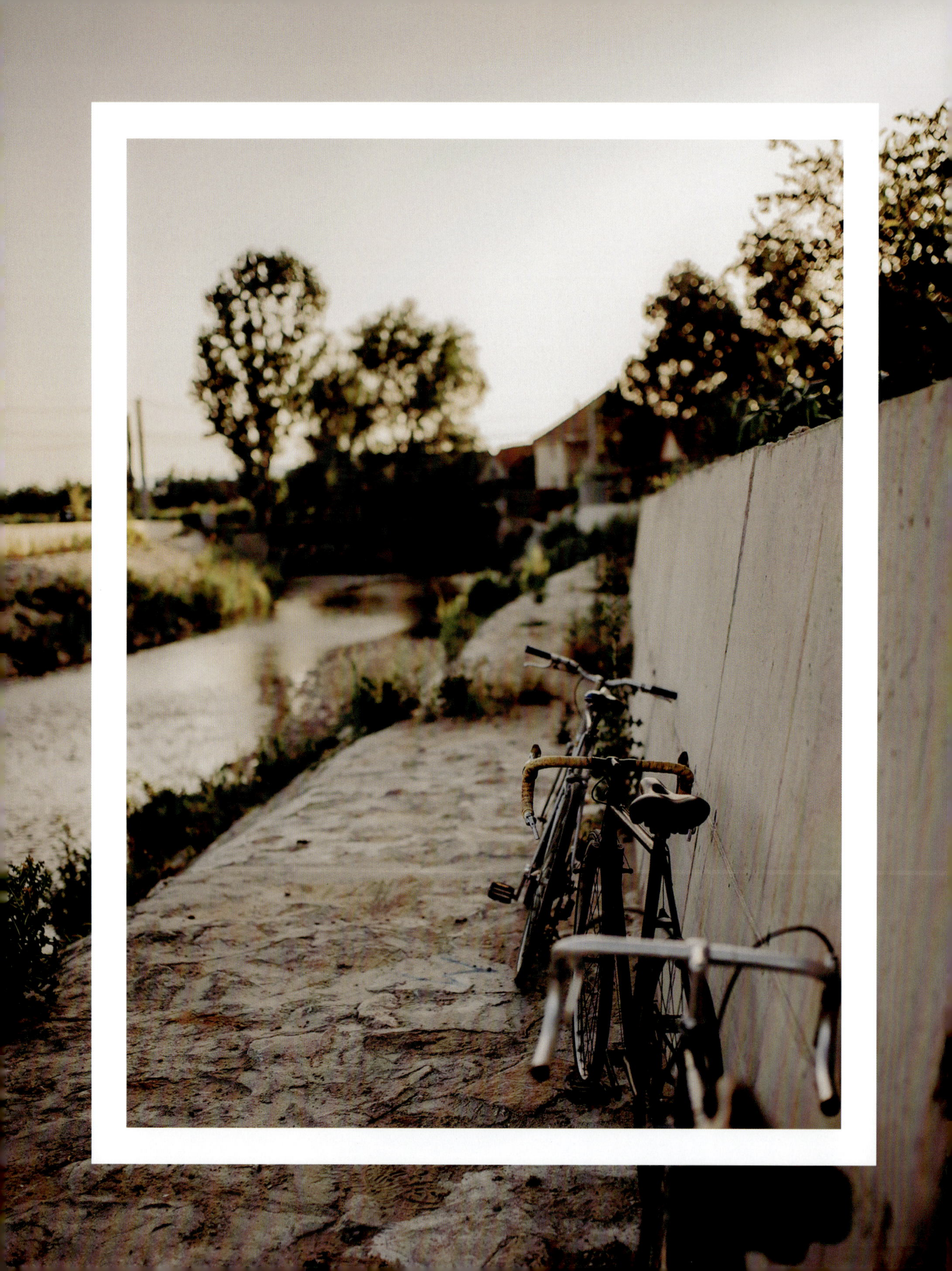

01

DAY ONE	15
MEMORY VERSE	33
WEEKLY REFLECTION	34

02

DAY ONE	37
MEMORY VERSE	57
WEEKLY REFLECTION	58

03

DAY ONE	61
MEMORY VERSE	81
WEEKLY REFLECTION	82

WORD STUDY: *QEDEM*	85
HABAKKUK & THE PSALMS	86
IMAGERY OF GOD'S POWER	88
FLOW OF CONTENT	89
THE 5 WOES	90
WHAT IS THE GOSPEL?	92

WEEK 1

READ THE BOOK OF HABAKKUK

DAY 1

1   After reading the entire book of Habakkuk, what key words and themes stand out to you?

2   What verse stands out to you the most?

3   What did you observe about the character of God in the book of Habakkuk?

4   Write out a prayer asking God to show you more of who He is through your study of Habakkuk.

WEEK 1 / DAY 2

GOD'S FAITHFULNESS TO HIS PEOPLE
IS PRESENT ON EVERY PAGE OF
THE OLD TESTAMENT.

Introduction to Habakkuk

HABAKKUK 1-3

If you are anything like most people, you probably have not read the book of Habakkuk recently. Maybe you have read it if you have read through the Bible in a year, or maybe you have read some cross-references that landed you in this book. Habakkuk is a tiny book of only three chapters that is tucked near the end of the Old Testament. It is so small that you might need the table of contents to locate this little book that is easy to flip past. Even though Habakkuk is not one of the most well-known books of the Bible, it contains a powerful message that was important, not only for the people in Habakkuk's own day but that is just as vital for us. Habakkuk contains a timeless question about the sovereignty and goodness of God in a world where devastation, corruption, and suffering seem to abound. If God is good, why do bad things happen? This is the question that the book of Habakkuk answers for us.

In the book of Habakkuk, we will get a glimpse into the prayer life of Habakkuk and see the questions he brings to God. We will also see the answer of the Lord and the assurance of God's goodness and trustworthiness.

It will be helpful for us before we begin to have a little refresher on the Old Testament history up until this point so that we can know exactly where we are in the story of Scripture as we open up the book of Habakkuk.

Scripture began in Genesis 1 as God made the world and everything in it. But by Genesis 3, sin enters the world at the fall. Though the consequence of Adam and Eve's sin in the garden was death, God made a promise that a Redeemer would come.

They did not know when or how, but God promised them that His plan that was set before the ages began would come to pass. In Genesis 12, we are introduced to a man named Abraham, and God makes a covenant with him and promises him that the Messiah would come from his line and that all nations would find blessing in his seed. Eventually, the people of Israel would be enslaved in Egypt, but God would faithfully deliver them and make a covenant with Moses. There were promises of blessing for obedience and consequences for disobedience (Genesis 19:3-6). When the people finally entered the Promised Land, there were judges and kings who would lead them. And God made a covenant with one king in particular. To David, God promised that a king would come through David's line who would sit on the throne forever (2 Samuel 7:8-16). God's faithfulness to His people is present on every page of the Old Testament. Sadly, we cannot say the same for the people. Despite God's steadfast love and faithfulness, the people rebelled against His gracious hand (2 Kings 17:5-15), and the people would be sent into captivity as a result of their sin (2 Chronicles 36:15-20). The book of Habakkuk takes place after the fall of the northern kingdom of Israel, but before the fall of the southern kingdom of Judah.

When we come to Habakkuk, it is important for us to understand that the northern kingdom had fallen nearly a century before. Habakkuk's prophecy here is looking ahead to the very similar destiny of the southern kingdom. Habakkuk is asking God why He would allow Judah to be overtaken by the wicked Babylonians. We do not know the exact dates of Habakkuk's ministry, but most scholars believe it to have been sometime between 640 and

597 BC, and the majority narrow it down even more to between 605-597 BC. This would place Habakkuk at the end of King Josiah's reign or the beginning of Jehoiakim's reign. Josiah had been a good king, and the nation had even experienced a mini-revival under his leadership. But the people were slipping farther and farther away from the Lord and under Jehoiakim, oppression reigned in the place of justice and mercy that was prevalent under the godly Josiah.

When we come to the book of Habakkuk and read about the state of God's people and the evil in the surrounding nations, we are left longing for the Messiah. The failures of Israel's kings lead us to long for a true and better king. But Habakkuk does not leave us hopeless. Instead, we walk away from the book with a renewed sense of hope in the sovereign and almighty hand of our God who works all things for the good of His people and to the glory of His name. We rest in that truth.

IF GOD IS GOOD, WHY DO BAD THINGS HAPPEN?

THIS IS THE QUESTION THAT THE BOOK OF

HABAKKUK ANSWERS FOR US.

1 As you read through the entire book of Habakkuk again, what new observations do you have?

_____
_____
_____
_____
_____
_____
_____
_____

2 How does the context of the book of Habakkuk in the story of Scripture help you to understand its message?

_____
_____
_____
_____
_____
_____
_____
_____

3 How does the book of Habakkuk make us long for the Messiah?

_____
_____
_____
_____
_____
_____
_____
_____

WEEK 1

HE IS ALWAYS FAITHFUL TO HIS COVENANT

DAY 3

The Message of Habakkuk

HABAKKUK 1-3

Can we trust God? Is He really good? These questions provide the foundation of the book of Habakkuk. But more than that, these questions are echoing through every book of the Bible. These are the questions that Satan planted in the heart of Eve from the earliest moments of Genesis 3. Satan tempted her by asking her if what God said was true. He twisted God's words and sought to make Eve question Her good and gracious Creator. Since then, humanity has been asking this same question even when they do not verbalize it. Is God good? Is His way best for us? Can we trust Him, or should we try to live in our own strength? Is He holding out on us? Why is this world full of suffering and sorrow?

Maybe you have asked these questions, or maybe you have been afraid to ask these questions. In the book of Habakkuk, we see the prayers and laments of Habakkuk as he speaks to God and takes his questions to the Lord. We also see in Habakkuk the way that the Lord answers Habakkuk's questions. The answer to Habakkuk's questions can help us see God's character and understand the answers to these questions that we have as well.

The structure of the book is two sets of questions from Habakkuk followed by answers from the Lord. The book then ends with a psalm of Habakkuk's that encourages our hearts to trust the Lord, even when we do not understand His ways.

Most of the prophets called the people of God to covenant obedience, but Habakkuk is very different. At first it seems that Habakkuk is calling God to covenant obedience, but ultimately, we see that Habakkuk's prayers served to teach Habakkuk and us as well. We learn that God's ways are not always our ways, but He is always faithful to His covenant. So though at first glance, we may think that God is not acting in accordance with His covenant or His character, in the end we will learn that He is.

The questions of Habakkuk remind us of another man who faced great difficulty and questioned the goodness and sovereignty of God. The style of Habakkuk's lament is very similar to that of Job. And in the end, the result is the same. Habakkuk, like Job, will learn to worshipfully submit to the Lord.

Habakkuk reminds us that God is good and gracious, while also being holy and just. Habakkuk points us to the cross because it is there that God's goodness and grace and His holiness and justice are perfectly displayed. It is there that Jesus bore the sins of His people and died under the justice and wrath of God in our place. And it is there that God's grace and goodness were poured out for us. This is the hope that we cling to as we read the book of Habakkuk. Our gracious and loving God will never desert His covenant, and He will never forsake His people.

Our lives are filled with sorrow and suffering, but the book of Habakkuk teaches us that God uses all things, including our sorrow and suffering, to bring glory to His name and sanctify His people. Through it all, we choose to worship when we do not understand and cling to our sovereign and gracious God.

---

1. Write a summary of the book of Habakkuk.

2 In what ways are we prone to question God's goodness as we look at the world around us?

3 How can we cling to the truths of His Word even when we do not understand?

4 Why do you think we need the message of Habakkuk today?

WEEK 1 / DAY 4

YET STILL,
HABAKKUK PRAYED.

How Long, O Lord?

HABAKKUK 1:1-4

The prophecy of Habakkuk is very unique among the prophetic books. Instead of simply sharing for us a monologue from the prophet, we are given insight into a dialogue between God and Habakkuk. The first verse of the book identifies this as an oracle of Habakkuk. An oracle was also commonly known as a burden. It was a heavy and weighty message. It is also interesting to note that this message is one that Habakkuk not only heard, but one that he saw, which he conveys through vivid imagery.

The book starts with the prayer and pleading of Habakkuk. He is in anguish over the sin that is around him and over what seems like silence from the Lord. Habakkuk's prayer begins with a common phrase of lament: how long? This lament phrase was used often, specifically in the psalms (Psalm 80:4, 13:1-2, etc.). These words of lament were an overflow of emotions from hearts that were yearning for God to hear, see, and know the plight of His people. Though the phrase is found throughout the psalms, this theme of lament is particularly found in Psalm 22, which was quoted by Jesus on the cross. This is a messianic psalm, and it is a reminder to us that Habakkuk is pointing us to Jesus. Jesus is the true and better Habakkuk. Habakkuk pleaded with the Father over the violence in his own day; Jesus pleaded these words to the Father in the midst of the greatest act of violence ever committed. As Habakkuk is a prophetic mediator between the people and God, Jesus is the mediator between God and His people. On the cross, Jesus echoed the question of Habakkuk, but through the cross, Jesus provided the answer. As we study the book of Habakkuk and see Habakkuk's weakness and strength, we are left longing for our perfect prophet, priest, and king.

Habakkuk's cry for Judah comes in the context of a solemn warning that had been given to the people in 1 Samuel 8:18. Israel had demanded a king like the other nations, and God had warned them about the consequences that would come from their actions. They insisted in their demands, and the Lord eventually gave to them what they had asked. In Habakkuk's day, the kingdom was divided, and Israel had already fallen. The people were paying for their decision to defy the words of the Lord through Samuel.

As Habakkuk looks around, the situation seems so hopeless. Violence, injustice, and destruction seem to be everywhere he looks. He is grieved. His heart is breaking because of the sin in the world around him and because the Lord seems far away. Habakkuk was a faithful man, and this prayer would not have been the first of its kind that he prayed. But to Habakkuk, it seemed that all his prayers went unanswered. Violence still reigned. The law was discarded. And the people were turning away from the Lord. Yet still, Habakkuk prayed. He prayed because God answers. And though he did not know how or when the answer would come, He knew the Scriptures, and He knew God's faithful.

Habakkuk's prayer is a plea with the Lord and an observation of what was happening around him. All around him was violence and disorder. Sin was everywhere he turned. Even those who were supposed to be serving the Lord were unjust and serving only themselves. Unity was nowhere to be found. Habakkuk's prayer even tells us that the law was paralyzed by the sin and wickedness of the people. They did not turn to the Lord because they were worshiping themselves. They did not think they needed the law at all. Justice is the law of God rightly applied, so with the discarding of the law came the discarding of justice. The poor and the weak were oppressed by the powerful, and the wicked were so numerous that they surrounded and outnumbered the righteous remnant. Even the religious leaders were corrupt. Habakkuk was a righteous man in the midst of an evil people and unjust leaders. With just a small remnant of faithful followers of Yahweh, he was outnumbered. Yet, he comes to the Lord. He pours out his heart. He prays, he pleads, and he waits.

Habakkuk knew who the Lord was, but the character of God did not seem to match the situation in front of his eyes. At some point in our lives, we will need to reconcile our theology and our experience. We will have to wrestle with the evil in the world when we serve a good God. This is exactly what Habakkuk is about. And in those moments when we do not understand where God is or what He is doing, we will be tempted to change our theology to align with what is happening in the world. And in those moments, we must stand strong on the truth of the Word of God and the goodness of His character. In those moments, we must not interpret God's Word through the lens of our circumstances, but we must interpret our circumstances through the lens of God's Word. And ultimately, it is in those moments that we must trust the sovereign hand of God that is working in ways we cannot see.

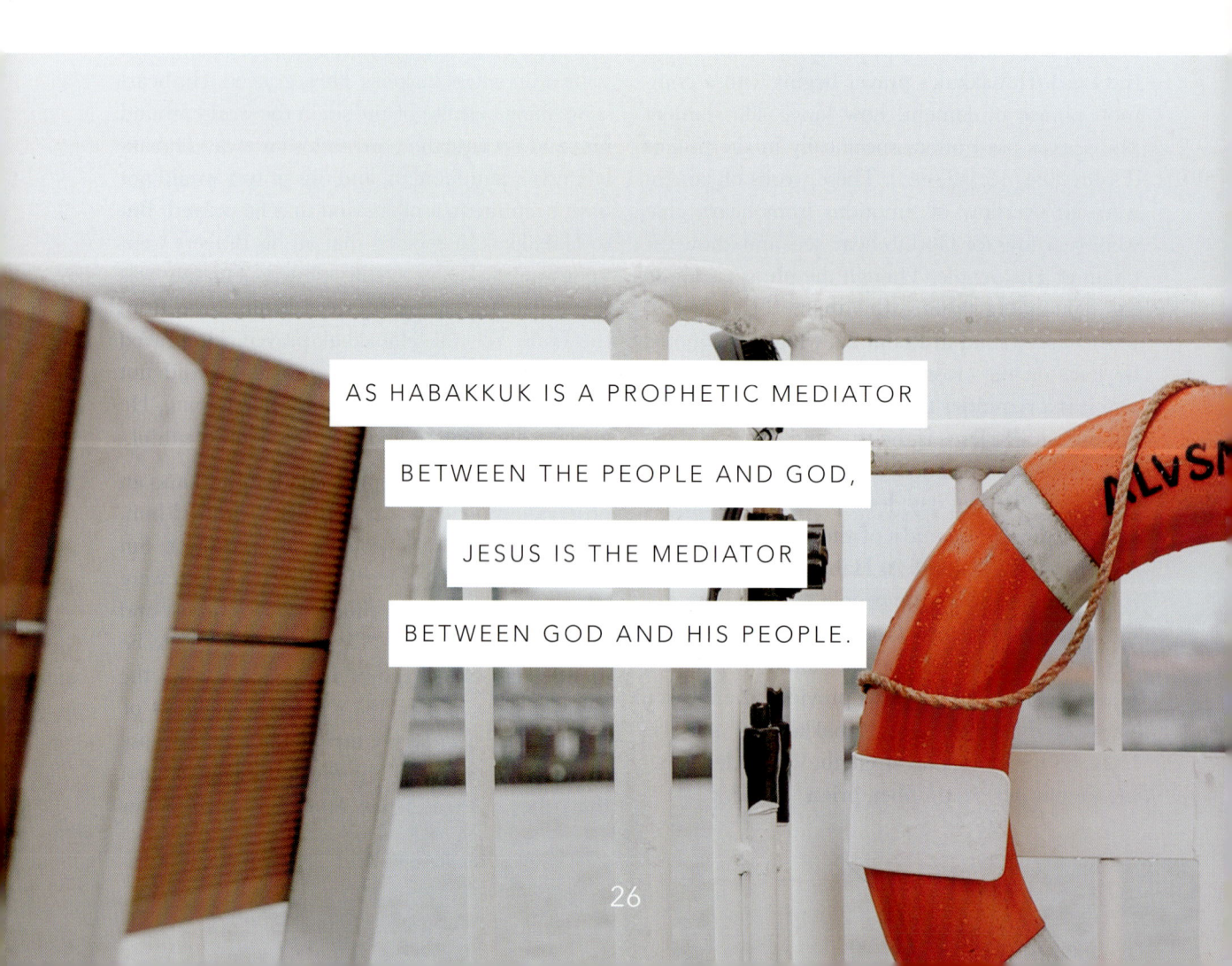

AS HABAKKUK IS A PROPHETIC MEDIATOR BETWEEN THE PEOPLE AND GOD, JESUS IS THE MEDIATOR BETWEEN GOD AND HIS PEOPLE.

1 Paraphrase Habakkuk 1:2-4.

2 What are the emotions that you think Habakkuk was feeling based on the questions he was asking? How have you experienced these same emotions and questions?

3 How does the gospel provide the answer to these questions?

Babylonians. We deserve the wrath of God, but God in His mercy has not given us what we deserved. God in His grace poured out the judgment that we deserved on Jesus. In Acts 13:3-52, we see Paul preaching in the synagogue and telling the story of all of the Old Testament while he proclaims the gospel. Tucked in verse 41 is a quote from Habakkuk 1:5. Paul reminds the Jews in Jerusalem that the judgment of the prophets would come upon those who rejected the Lord. But the good news is this: even in their rejection, the gospel would go forth to the gentiles. Look and see. Wonder and be astonished at what God is doing. He is calling His people, not just from the Jews but from every tribe, tongue, and nation. Because of Jesus, we are free from the wrath that we deserve. It has been placed on Jesus, and we have been showered in His grace.

And yet, in this life, we still do not always understand how God is working. We find ourselves feeling like Habakkuk. We do not always get this inside information like Habakkuk did, but we know that this truth remains. God is working in ways we do not know and in ways that we do not understand. Even in the bleakest situations, God is working. Ephesians 3:20 declares with confidence that God is doing more than we could ever ask or think.

When things seem bad, He is working. When we do not understand, He is working. When His ways do not make sense to us, we rest in His sovereignty and truth in His grace. He is good, and He will work for the good of His people and the glory of His name.

HE IS WORKING IN WAYS

THAT ONLY HE CAN.

1 What do we learn about the character of God in this passage?

2 How can this passage provide us hope when it does not seem like God is working?

3 Read Isaiah 55:8-9. How does this passage help us understand God's response?

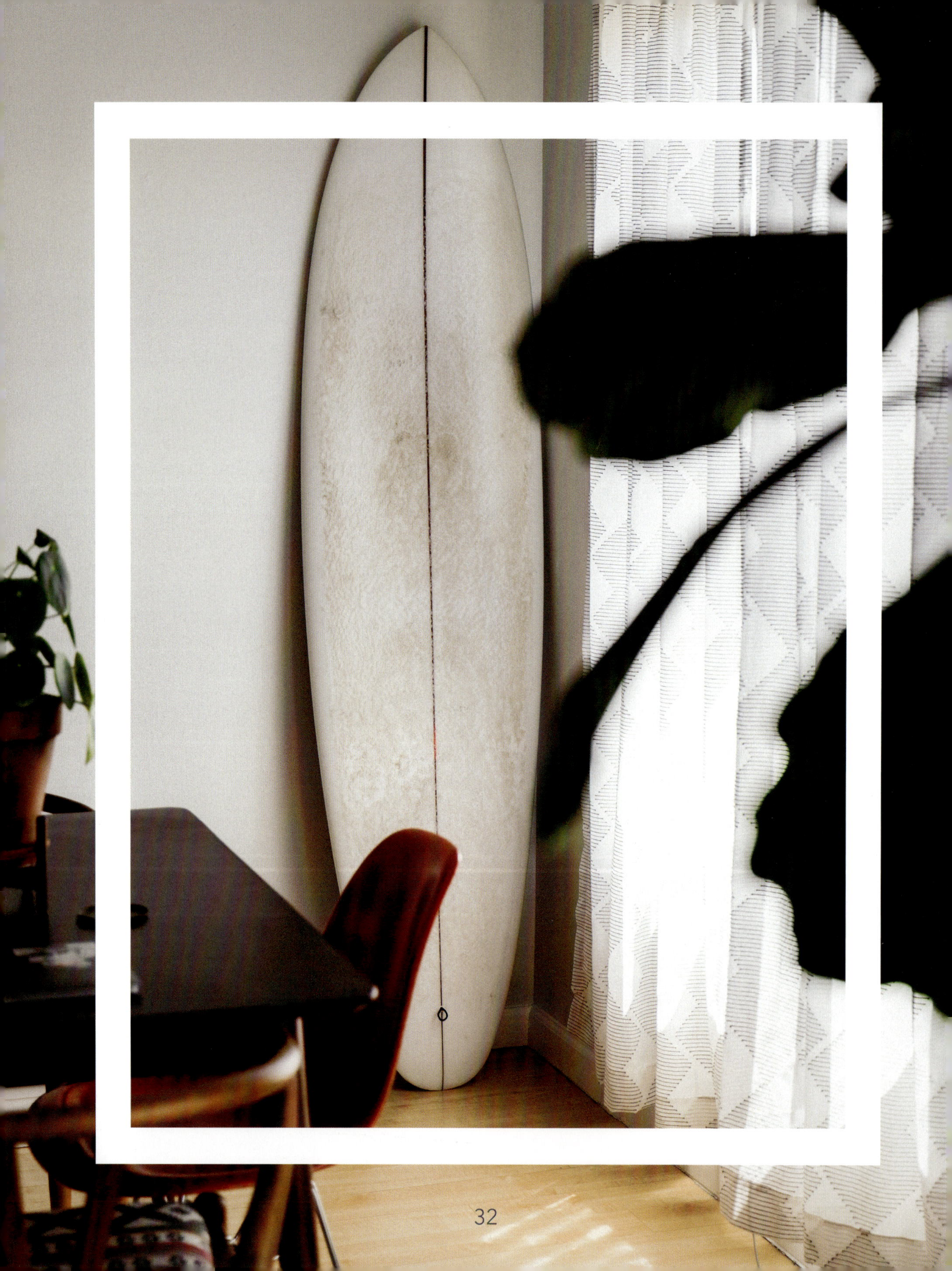

01   MEMORY VERSE

Though the fig tree does not bud and there is no fruit on the vines, though the olive crop fails and the fields produce no food, though the flocks disappear from the pen and there are no herds in the stalls

Habakkuk 3:17

Week One Reflection

Paraphrase the passage from this week.

_____
_____
_____
_____
_____
_____
_____
_____

What did you observe from this week's text about God and His character?

_____
_____
_____
_____
_____
_____
_____
_____

What does this passage reveal about the condition of mankind and yourself?

_____
_____
_____
_____
_____
_____
_____
_____

Habakkuk 1:1-11

How does this passage point to the gospel?

_____
_____
_____
_____
_____
_____
_____
_____

How should you respond to this passage? What specific action steps can you take this week to apply this passage?

_____
_____
_____
_____
_____
_____
_____
_____

Write a prayer in response to your study of God's Word. Adore God for who He is, confess sins that He revealed in your own life, ask Him to empower you to walk in obedience, and pray for anyone who comes to mind as you study.

_____
_____
_____
_____
_____
_____
_____
_____

WEEK 2

HE IS FROM EVERLASTING AND TO EVERLASTING

DAY 1

Everlasting Lord

HABAKKUK 1:12

In chapter 1, Habakkuk had come prayerfully pleading for the Lord to see and act, and God had answered. The answer though is not what Habakkuk was likely anticipating. In today's passage, we see one of the key verses of the book of Habakkuk. Habakkuk still had questions, and he is about to ask them of the Lord. But first, he turns to the Lord in adoration. He is reminding Himself of the Lord's steadfast character. Habakkuk is still wrestling through his current circumstances and what he knows to be true.

His reaction of adoration reminds us of the character of our God and urges us to respond to our own trials with our hearts centered on the unshakable character of our God.

Habakkuk first turns to the eternal nature of God. God is everlasting. Though the problems on Habakkuk's heart were bound by time and place, God is not bound. He is from everlasting to everlasting. He has no beginning and no end. His perspective is far bigger than our own. He sees what we cannot see and knows what we cannot know. The eternality of God is a comfort to us as people who do not even know what tomorrow will bring. The comfort for us is that we do not know what lies ahead, but our God does.

Habakkuk then addresses God as LORD. This is the covenant name of God. It is the name Yahweh, which was so holy to the Jewish people that they would not even speak this name out loud. Habakkuk breaths the covenant name of God in His prayer, knowing that the God who made a covenant with His people is a God who will also keep the covenant that He has made. Part of God's covenant with His people promised He would send the Messiah through the line of David. This was the promise to which the people of God clung. This is what all of the Old Testament looks forward to. As Habakkuk processed the word of the Lord that he had just heard, it is likely that his heart was wondering and questioning how all that God had promised would take place. If Judah was destroyed, how could the Messiah come. He did not understand. But He knew that God was a God of covenant and that He would not forsake His promises to His people.

"My God" and my "Holy One" are the next names that Habakkuk gives to the Lord. These names reflect the nearness and the all-surpassing greatness of the Lord. He is holy. He is set apart from all others. He is spotless and perfect. He is so much different than we are. And yet the people of God can say that He is ours. He is our God. Though He is high and holy, He is also close to His children. This is a great comfort for us in moments that we do not understand what He is doing because we know that what He is doing is good. And we know that while He is doing it, He will be close.

Habakkuk still does not understand, and yet he knows that God's covenant people will not die out. God will never abandon His promises. He will be faithful to every last detail. As Habakkuk considers that God has ordained the Babylonians for judgment on Judah, he also recognizes that the Lord is the Rock of His people. He is the firm foundation when life seems shaken and unsteady. His character is the bedrock of our faith. We do not place our truth in our circumstances but in our God. We do not trust what our eyes can see, but we trust the God who rules it all.

As we look to Jesus, we are reminded that the character of God, which Habakkuk was clinging to, proved to be true. God kept His promises to bring the Messiah. It did not happen how people may have expected, but God was perfectly faithful to His promises. And the events of the book of Habakkuk were laying the foundation for the fulfillment of that promise.

In our own lives, there will be times when we do not understand what God is doing. There will be moments when our situation does not seem to align with what we know to be true of God. It is in those moments that we can come honestly to the Lord in prayer and preach the gospel to our own hearts. It is then that we need to remind ourselves of the character of our God and trust not in our circumstances but in our God.

HE SEES WHAT WE CANNOT SEE AND KNOWS WHAT WE CANNOT KNOW.

1 What do we learn about God's character from Habakkuk's words?

2 How should this verse encourage us to go to the Lord in prayer?

3 Can you think of a situation in your own life that you do not understand? How does God's character comfort you?

WEEK 2 / DAY 2

SIN IS NOT HIDDEN
FROM THE LORD.

I Will Watch

HABAKKUK 1:13-2:1

Habakkuk has declared the character of God, but his heart is still struggling. His prayer is raw and vulnerable. We do not see in any way a sense of masking what he is feeling or hiding his heart from the Lord. He comes humble and broken before the throne of the Almighty. He does not understand, but He will wait for God to answer.

Habakkuk continues with speaking of God's character by pointing out that the Lord is pure. Purity was vitally important in Israel as their temple ceremonies included ceremonial cleansing to make the people pure before the pure and holy Lord. But as Habakkuk reflects on God's purity, he is confused. If God is pure, why does He look on sin? Initially, Habakkuk says that God cannot look on sin, but then he realizes that God does look on sin. Sin is not hidden from the Lord. The Babylonians have committed great sin before the Lord, and they will continue to do so. But Habakkuk is asking, "Why does God allow it?"

Habakkuk knows that God is sovereign. And if God is sovereign over all things, then He has allowed this to happen. As hard as he tries, Habakkuk cannot seem to understand why. It seemed like Judah was being treated like the lowly fish of the sea, while the Babylonians were like violent fishermen who would mercilessly kill anyone in their path. So Habakkuk was wondering about the covenant. He had called the Lord by His covenant name, and he desperately wanted to know if God would be faithful. From his strong declarations of God's character, it certainly seemed that deep down Habakkuk knew that God would be faithful, but in the moment, His heart was burdened and weary. Many assume from some of the language of Habakkuk that Habakkuk worked in the temple, perhaps as a temple prophet or musician. His pleadings are reminiscent of the psalms. Perhaps as he prayed, he remembered the words of psalm after psalm that declared God's goodness. Perhaps he remembered the words of a psalm like Psalm 18:30, which declares that God's ways are perfect. Perhaps he remembered the faithfulness of God to Job when nothing made sense.

In the opening verse of chapter 2, Habakkuk declares that he will stand at his watchpost. He will watch, and he will wait. The watchman was a sentinel in Old Testament times. He would stand in the watchtower on the lookout for what was coming. Prophets were often referenced as watchmen who were able to warn the people, give the words of the Lord, and see what was ahead. But part of the watchman's job was simply to watch and wait. So Habakkuk took his place as he prayed, and he was still before the Lord. He was watching and waiting for what God would do. Would God be faithful to His people? Would God keep His covenant? Would justice be served? Would evil be conquered?

If Habakkuk could have seen from his watchtower far into the future on the nearby hill of Calvary, he would have known the answer to every question that burdened his heart that day. Though judgment was coming for their sin, God would be faithful to His people by sending the promised Messiah. He would keep His covenant and bring with Jesus a new covenant better than the last. Justice would be served when the sinless Son of God paid the price for the sins of His own. And evil would be conquered as redemption was accomplished and Jesus breathed, "It is finished," from the cross. God's faithfulness would ultimately be displayed in Jesus.

We, like Habakkuk, often find ourselves in situations that we do not understand. We feel the weight of living in a broken and sinful world. We see the impact of the fall everywhere around us. We wonder why God allows evil in this world. Our hearts yearn to know that God will be faithful to us. As we watch and as we wait for the Lord, we too must shift our gaze to Calvary and fix our eyes on Jesus. It is at Calvary that we see the love of God poured out for us. It is there that we know His faithful love for us. There will be moments when we do not understand, and in those moments, our God is near. As we wait and as we watch and as we wrestle with prayer and cry out in tears, we know that God has come near to us. He

THOUGH JUDGMENT WAS COMING FOR THEIR SIN, GOD WOULD BE FAITHFUL TO HIS PEOPLE BY SENDING THE PROMISED MESSIAH.

will be faithful because that is who He is.

1 How is God's character comforting to us when we do not understand our circumstances?

___

2 How does remembering God's faithfulness in the past encourage us for our current situations?

___

3 How can we watch and wait for the Lord?

___

WEEK 2

HE WOULD ACCOMPLISH THAT WHICH HE HAD PROMISED

DAY 3

Wait in Faith

HABAKKUK 2:2-5

Habakkuk was watching and waiting for God to answer. And in today's passage, we are told that God did indeed answer. The time frame between Habakkuk 2:1 and Habakkuk 2:2 is unknown to us. We do not know how long Habakkuk had to wait for God to speak, but at the start of verse 2, we are encouraged that the Lord answered the cry of His servant. God was not silent.

God's answer came in the form of a command and a message of hope. God would be faithful. God spoke to Habakkuk and told him to write down the vision on tablets so that it could be preserved and remembered. God was about to say something very important. Not only would this message be important for Habakkuk, but it would be important for all people of all time. These words were a timeless promise that rested not in the circumstances of the day but in the timeless and eternal character of God. These words would stand the test of time. The last line of verse 2 is an interesting phrase in the original Hebrew that says that he who reads it may run. The word translated as "run" means "to herald," and this phrasing of running with a message was often used of the prophets who ran to tell the message of God. Here it is, the gospel message that God's people are called to herald and preach to those around them. It is the message that God will keep His Word and that the just will live by faith. It is the same message that we are called to proclaim today.

God's Word will come to pass. This is the comfort that was proclaimed to Habakkuk and the comfort that should overwhelm our hearts as we read these words. Verse 3 reminds us that God will be faithful. Habakkuk had received news that things in Judah were going to get bad as the Babylonians came in, but God's plans would not be thwarted. Even this judgment would serve to fulfill God's sovereign purposes. Verse 3 reminds us of the trustworthiness and reliability of God's Word. God's plan was pressing forward. They would be fulfilled at the appointed time. Nothing and no one could interfere with what God was doing. God's plan was moving forward, and God who is truth does not lie to His people. God's Word can be trusted. His promises are sure. He will never fail His people.

Habakkuk knew that the judgment of the Lord was coming. He struggled to grasp what God was doing, but God came to him with words of comfort. God whispered to Habakkuk that He could be trusted. Habakkuk likely had the same kind of questions that Abraham and Sarah had as they waited for a promised child (Genesis 12-21). How could God's promises come about if this was their situation? For Abraham and Sarah, God had promised a child, but they were old and barren. For Habakkuk, God had promised His faithfulness and a Messiah, but Judah was coming under God's judgment, and the Babylonians would soon attack. How would God bring His promises to pass? The Lord said that His plan was hastening or testifying to the end. In Hebrew, the idea is that of breath. God was breathing out His plan. He was active and not passive. He would accomplish that which He had promised. God could be counted on to do what He said.

The end of verse 3 is a beautiful promise. God's Word would come about. There will be times when it seems that God is moving slowly. And in those times, God's people would have to wait. There would be times it would seem like God was late, but He never misses His appointments. There would be times that God's people would question whether it would happen at all. But it would. Just as surely as the sun rises every morning, God will be faithful to His Word.

The Septuagent (also known as the LXX) is the Greek translation of the Hebrew Old Testament. It translates the end of verse 3 slightly differently, and it is interesting for us to note. It translates the word "it" as the word "he." This translation brings out for us what the awaited promise was that the people awaited—the promise of the Messiah. It was Jesus. The author of Hebrews understood it this way as well when he quoted this passage in Hebrews 10:37-38. This promise that God's people were clinging to and hoping for was the promise of their deliverer. And He would surely come.

There would be moments when God's people would wonder. There would be moments when God's plans seemed slow. But God would fulfill His promise.

As believers today, we know that God did fulfill that promise. He sent Jesus to rescue and redeem His own. God was faithful all along the way. And yet we also wait for the final fulfillment of this promise, for we still wait for Jesus to return. We wait for the end that all of time hastens toward (1 Corinthians 15:24-26). We await our Savior to return and for the final and full fulfillment of every promise. The people of God are characterized by waiting. We are a people who wait for our God. In the waiting, we may not always understand. And yet we can trust Him. We lean on His Word and know that God is accomplishing His purposes at this very moment in ways that we cannot see or comprehend. And, in the end, we as His people choose to trust Him. We rest in His faithfulness and lean on His grace.

GOD'S PLANS WOULD NOT BE THWARTED.

1 We are not sure how much time passed between verses 1 and 2. What does this teach you about your own season of waiting?

2 How does this passage encourage you to trust God's Word?

3 What does this passage teach you about God's character?

WEEK 2 / DAY 4

THE PEOPLE OF GOD ARE MADE
RIGHTEOUS BY FAITH, AND IT IS
BY FAITH THAT WE LIVE.

The Righteous By Faith Shall Live

HABAKKUK 2:4

In the previous verses, the Lord began His answer to Habakkuk. He answered Habakkuk's pleading with a reminder of His character and the assurance that what He had said would come about. Habakkuk, along with all who would read the words of the prophecy, were urged to trust and wait because the Lord would be faithful to His Word.

Today's verse is a theme verse of the book of Habakkuk and a verse that encapsulates in just a few words one of the main themes of the Bible. Here in Habakkuk 2:4, God contrasts for us the life of an unbeliever and the life of a believer. In these timeless words, we are reminded of who we were, who we are, and what God desires for us.

We find here a contrast that comes from the lips of the Lord. God speaks here of the Babylonians, but the description is true of every person apart from salvation. The unbeliever's soul is puffed up. This is the sin of pride, and it is the root of every other sin. All sin is rooted in our pride and self-sufficiency. We think that we have a better way. We think that we know better than God. This is the state of every person apart from Christ. The description continues by telling us that this person's soul is not upright. Their life is characterized by the deeds that flow from the pride of their hearts. This is a bleak picture, but there is hope.

The contrast of this description is God's description of His own. Just three short words in the Hebrew in an order that translates as "The righteous by faith shall live." These words are some of the most well-known in the Christian faith. Jewish rabbi's also have recognized these words and their vast importance as a type of distilling of the Law down to its most basic message. The Jewish Talmud records these words from Rabbi Simlai; "Moses gave Israel 613 commandments. David reduced them to eleven (see Psalm 15), Micah to three (Micah 6:8), Isaiah to two (Isaiah 56:1), but Habakkuk to one: "the righteous will live by his faith." This is the heart of Scripture and truly the heart of the gospel.

The people of God are made righteous by faith in God, and they live both now and for eternity because of their faith in God's finished work.

To be righteous is to be right with God, and that is only possible because of the work of Christ. For Old Testament believers like Habakkuk, they were putting their faith in the promised Messiah. They did not have all the details, and they didn't know how it would happen, but by faith they rested in the work of Jesus on the cross. We live on the other side of the cross. We place our faith in the finished work of Jesus on the cross just like the Old Testament believers, but for us, we are placing our faith in a past event. We are made righteous by God's justification of us. We are given the righteousness of Jesus in exchange for our sin. This is the beauty of the gospel.

The people of God are made righteous by faith, and it is by faith that we live. The life of God's people should be continually characterized by faith. This is a sweet reminder after God told Habakkuk to trust and wait. Trusting and waiting is what God has called His people to do. We live by faith and not by sight (2 Corinthians 5:7). We rest in our God and not in what we can see. These words are repeated three times throughout the New Testament (Romans 1:16-17, Galatians 3:11, Hebrews 10:36-39). These are gospel words that turn our eyes to Jesus.

These words point us to Jesus because it is only through Him that anyone can be made righteous. And it is only through Him that we are enabled to live the life of faith. It is because of Him that we know the abundant life to which God has called us (John 10:10). And it is Christ who walks with us every step of the way.

These words can spur us on to faithfulness in our ordinary lives. This is the rally cry of every child of God. We are made righteous by faith, and now we will live in faith.

TO BE RIGHTEOUS IS TO BE RIGHT WITH GOD, AND THAT IS ONLY POSSIBLE BECAUSE OF THE WORK OF CHRIST.

1 What are the differences between the person apart from Christ and the righteous person in this verse?

2 How is a person made righteous? How does this small verse point us to the gospel?

3 What does it mean to live by faith? How can you grow in your application of living by faith?

WEEK 2

GOD IS WITH US IN THE MIDST OF BROKENNESS

DAY 5

May The Earth Be Filled With His Glory

HABAKKUK 2:5-14

After the Lord has paused to encourage the faithful remnant and point us to the gospel of justification by faith, He returns with a message about the Babylonians. Verse 5 serves as a transition verse, reminding us again of the character (or lack thereof) of the Babylonians. The text then moves into a series of five woes to the Babylonians that are found in chapter 2. These woes are a reminder to us of God's care for justice. He is concerned with truth and justice, and He is at work in the world. Today's passage ends by pointing us forward to our eternal hope.

Today's passage covers three of the five woes against the Babylonians in chapter 2. The first speaks to the wickedness of those who were becoming wealthy dishonestly. But the Lord reminds us that this wealth is not secure. We see the words "how long" which seem to echo Habakkuk's opening prayer. The Lord is gently reminding us that though the wicked seem to prosper right now, it will not be forever.

The next woe is similar and speaks of those who gain unjustly. Yet it is also in these verses that we see that their injustice would be their undoing. God would not tolerate their wickedness. In their rebellion against the Lord, they would forfeit His blessing. The third woe reflects on a society that is built on violence and bloodshed. This mindset of conquering and bloodshed is not from the Lord, and they themselves would face judgment.

The woes are weighty, and yet it is easy to see some of these same characteristics in the world around us. Verse 14 gives the answer to the tragedy of the woes and fills our hearts with hope. The verse nearly seems out of place in the midst of warnings of judgment. In this verse is a promise that the entire earth will be filled with the knowledge of the glory of God. This intimate knowing of the Lord will be spread across the entire earth, just as the waters cover the sea.

The words may seem out of place at first reading, but they are not unique to this passage. We find similar promises in Numbers 14:21, Psalm 72:19, and Isaiah 11:9. This is a covenant promise given by a covenant-keeping God. This verse broadens the scope of the book of Habakkuk for us. This is not just about one moment in time or what would happen at the end of the reign of the Babylonians. This is an eschatological (or future) hope. This is the same hope we cling to today.

The wording here is interesting for us to note. This language of a filling with God's glory was used many times in the Old Testament, though not usually to refer to the earth. Instead, it was used to refer to God's glory filling the temple or tabernacle and God dwelling among His people (Exodus 40:34-35, 1 Kings 8:10-11, Ezekiel 10:3, Haggai 2:7). These were glorious moments in Scripture when God's glory descended to dwell in the holy place. But this promise is far bigger.

This is the promise of the whole earth being made into the Holy of Holies. This is the promise that we see fulfilled in Revelation 21 as the new heavens and new earth are revealed, and there is no temple because God dwells with man. It is the day for which we as believers wait. And yet, it is also something that we already experience, though not yet fully. God is with us and dwells with us and in us now. We are united to Christ, and we are never alone.

And just as this promise was given in the midst of brokenness, God is with us in the midst of brokenness. And we cling to this same promise. God will fulfill every word of His promises. He will be faithful.

HE IS CONCERNED WITH TRUTH AND JUSTICE, AND HE IS AT WORK IN THE WORLD.

1 What does this passage teach you about how justice is important to God?

_____
_____
_____
_____
_____
_____
_____

2 What does this passage teach you about God's character?

_____
_____
_____
_____
_____
_____
_____

3 How does this passage encourage you personally?

_____
_____
_____
_____
_____
_____
_____
_____

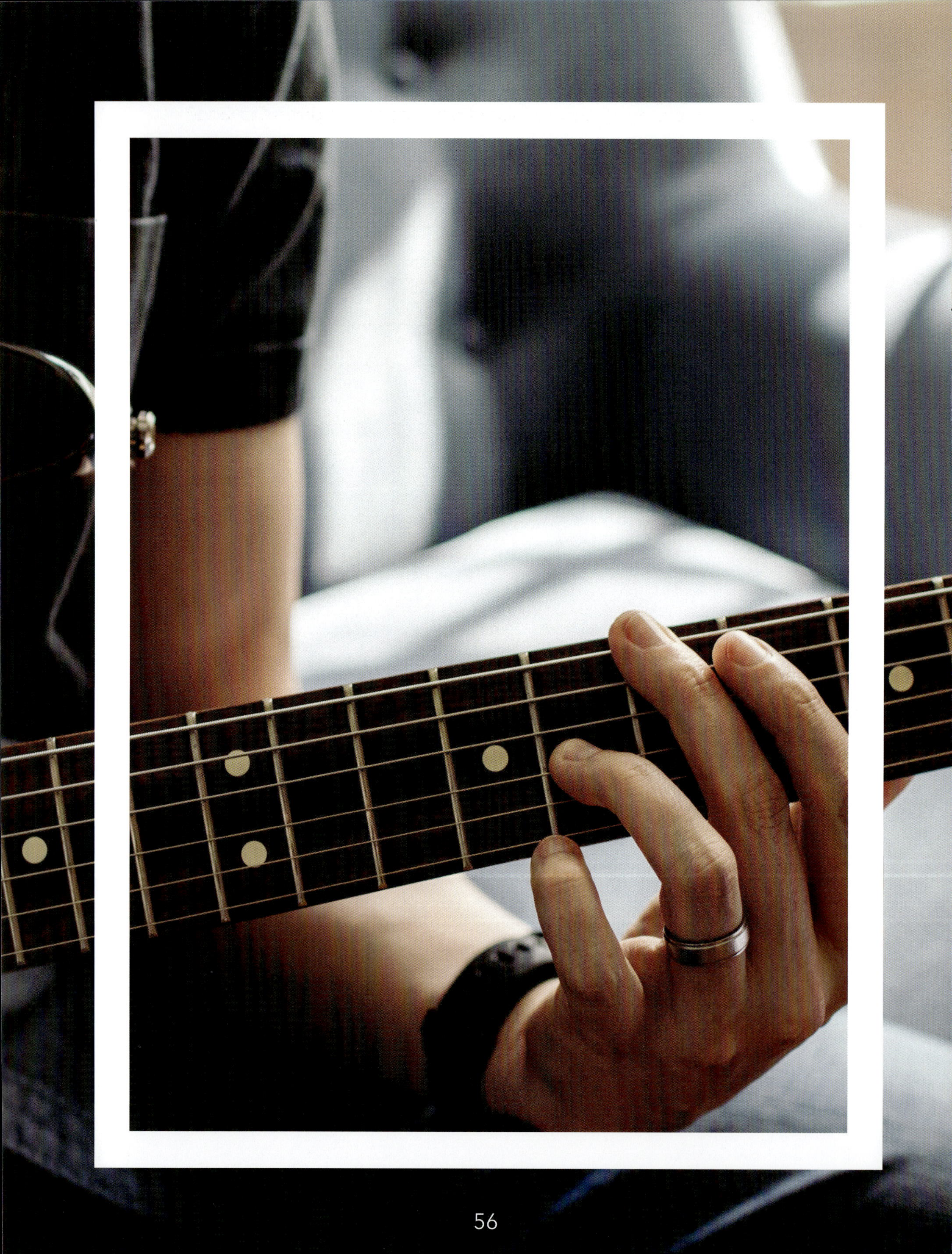

02 MEMORY VERSE

yet I will celebrate in the Lord; I will rejoice in the God of my salvation!

Habakkuk 3:18

Week Two Reflection

Paraphrase the passage from this week.

What did you observe from this week's text about God and His character?

What does this passage reveal about the condition of mankind and yourself?

Habakkuk 1:12 – 2:14

How does this passage point to the gospel?

How should you respond to this passage? What specific action steps can you take this week to apply this passage?

Write a prayer in response to your study of God's Word. Adore God for who He is, confess sins that He revealed in your own life, ask Him to empower you to walk in obedience, and pray for anyone who comes to mind as you study.

WEEK 3

THERE IS ONE WHO NEVER FAILS

DAY 1

God Is Still On His Throne

HABAKKUK 2:15-20

God is still on His throne. No matter what is happening in the world around us, our God is still in control. This is the hope of today's passage. These verses wrap up the last of the woes found in Habakkuk, and yet, in their midst, is great hope for the people of God and sweet reminders of His sovereign plan and rule. These verses are a reminder to us of the hope that is found in the Lord, no matter what the circumstances of our life or of our world are at the present time.

The first woe of today's passage is toward the Babylonians who make their neighbors drink and then shame them. This is an illustration for us of a devastating spiritual reality. The idea of getting another person drunk was seen (and often still is) as a way to control another person. At its most basic sense, it is an abuse of power. It is a way that an enemy can manipulate another person into lowering their inhibitions or declining to resist. The result here is devastating shame. Though this was likely happening in a literal sense, it was also a picture of what was happening as the Babylonians with all their power came in to manipulate, coerce, and shame the nations. But the promise of the Lord is that they will not get away with their sin. They will themselves experience the shame that they have tried to put on others.

The cup of the Lord's judgment is personified for us. Throughout the Old Testament, the cup is used as a symbol of God's holy wrath. Though the nations would drink from the cup of Babylon's wrath (Jeremiah 51:7), the Lord would be faithful to judge. God's wrath would be poured out at the appointed time. The justice and wrath of God are spoken often as a cup in passages like Psalm 75:8 that remind us that His justice will come.

But there is One who has taken the cup of God's wrath in the place of His people. In our sin, we too deserve the wrath of God. Yet, the New Testament presents for us a picture of the Promised One who drank the cup in our place (Mark 14:32-42). At the cross, Jesus bore the wrath of God in the place of His people. And through His sacrifice, our sin and shame are removed.

Through the power of the gospel, Jesus holds forth to His children another cup. This cup is the new covenant in His blood (Matthew 26:28). This is the cup of communion and not wrath. It is the cup we drink from as we celebrate the Lord's Supper and rehearse the goodness of Jesus and the beauty of the gospel. There are two cups. The cup of wrath and the cup of communion. For the people of God, the cup of wrath has been drunk by our Savior, and the cup of communion is held out to us because of His sacrifice.

The final woe speaks to the problem of idolatry. The Babylonians worshiped things they had made with their own hands. They were putting their trust in idols, and ultimately, they were trusting in themselves. Instead of trusting in their Creator, they trusted in things they had made with their own hands from the things He had created. But there was no salvation in these homemade gods. They had no power to save, no power to redeem, and no power to comfort. How often we too look to idols. We set up things and people, thinking that these will bring us the comfort and hope that we need. The things of this world will fail us every single time, but there is One who never fails.

The final verse of the chapter is a sweet reminder of God's sovereign hand. In spite of all that the Babylonians had done and were still to do, God was still and is still in control. The earth stands reverently before Him in worship. He has not slept for a moment, and He has not lost one ounce of control in the affairs of men. Neither the Babylonian's rebellion, nor Satan's schemes can stand against Him

Worship shifts our perspective. That is exactly what happened to Habakkuk. This vision of the Lord high and lifted up is going to silence his objections and shift his anguish to praise. Habakkuk has been reminded of who God is, and we need the same. We need to be reminded that our God is good and merciful. We need to be reminded that He is holy and just. We need to be reminded that in our weakness, Christ came. We need the gospel to change our perspective and point us to the cross.

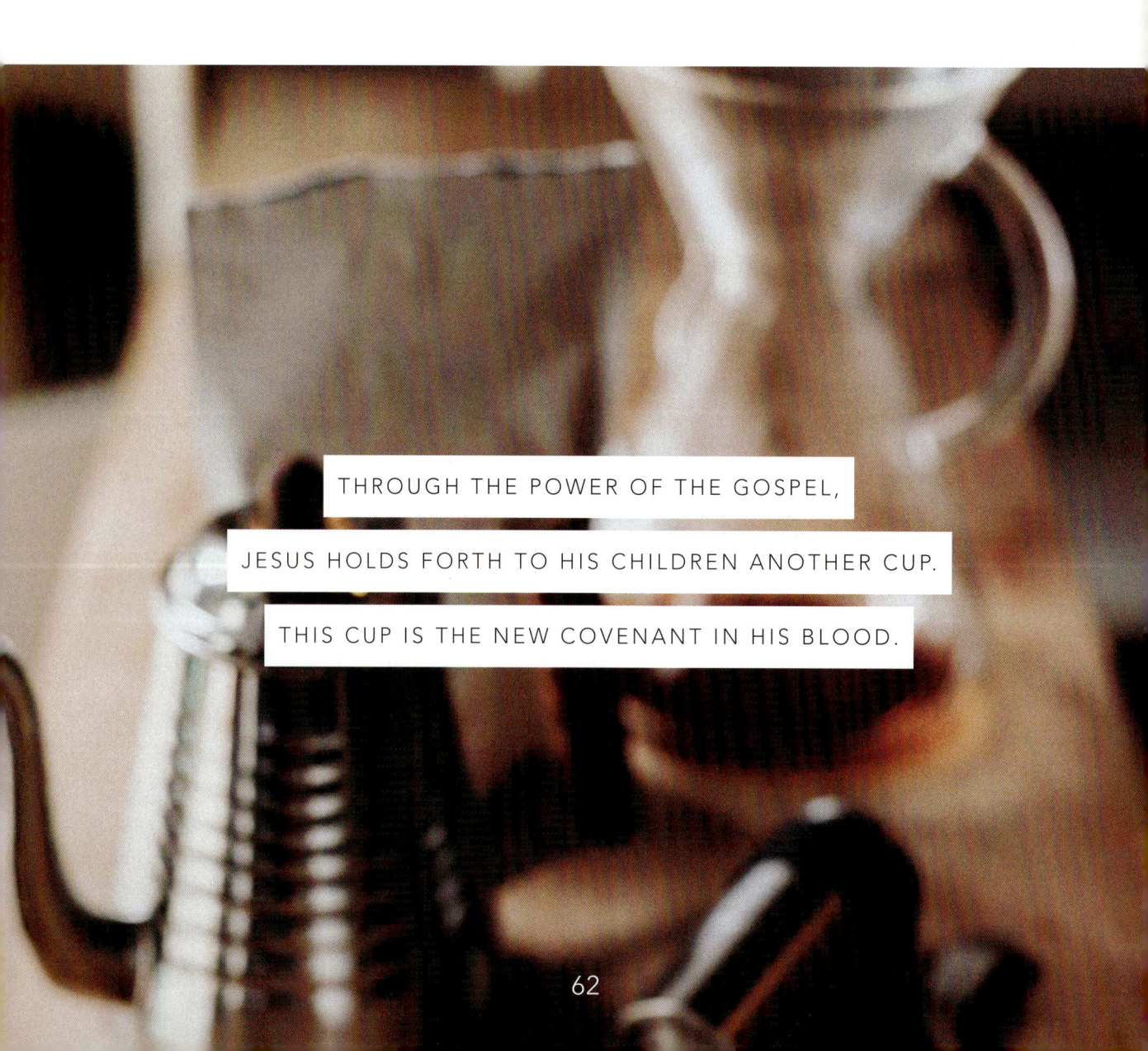

THROUGH THE POWER OF THE GOSPEL,

JESUS HOLDS FORTH TO HIS CHILDREN ANOTHER CUP.

THIS CUP IS THE NEW COVENANT IN HIS BLOOD.

1 What does this passage teach you about the character of God?

2 These verses speak a lot about idolatry. In what way is idolatry at the foundation of all sin?

3 How does a vision of who God is shift our perspective?

WEEK 3 / DAY 2

GOD POURS OUT MERCY.
THIS IS WHO HE IS.

Remember Mercy

HABAKKUK 3:1-2

The third and final chapter of Habakkuk is a prayer and a psalm. It is the words of a prophet who has seen the Lord and is left in awe of who God is and of the works of His hands. The prophet's prayer takes the form of a beautiful psalm that seems to have been a part of the liturgy of God's people. We even find three occurrences of the word *selah* in this psalm found outside of the book of Psalms. The chapter points to the character and works of God and ultimately, to the confidence that the prophet finds in the Lord. It does not put a bow on the hardship of the book or ignore the struggle. Instead, it turns us to the answer—the goodness of God.

Habakkuk reflects back on what he has heard and seen in this prophecy. The report of who God is and what He does is the Word of God and the plan of God. And when we see Him in His Word, it changes our perspective. At the beginning of the book of Habakkuk, the Lord had called for Habakkuk to look and see, to wonder and be astounded at what God is doing and who He is (Habakkuk 1:5). Here we see that Habakkuk has obeyed that command. The Word of the sovereign Lord had changed the heart of the prophet. This understanding of who God is and what He is doing brings to Habakkuk the fear of the Lord. It is this fear of the Lord that the book of Proverbs repeatedly tells us is the beginning of wisdom (Proverbs 9:10). The Lord spoke, and Habakkuk is humbled and in awe of who God is.

Habakkuk makes three requests in verse 2, and his prayer is a timeless one. To revive, reveal, and remember are the pleas of the prophet as he comes before the Lord. The events of the last chapters have caused Habakkuk to come humbly in prayer, but they have also allowed Him to come boldly in prayer to the eternal God.

Twice, Habakkuk references "these years" as he pleads with the Lord to act. Scholars differ on exactly what this references, but most conclude that it is a reference to this time period after the promise has been given of the coming Messiah and before the promise is fulfilled in Christ. It is this time of waiting. It is the in-between. On this side of the cross, we are also in a similar position to the people of God in the time of exile. Christ has come, and yet we wait until the final consummation of God's eternal plan. We cry out with Habakkuk as we wait.

Habakkuk's prayer is for God to revive. He wants the Lord to be faithful as He has always been. He wants God to be who He is. He is praying in alignment with God's righteous and faithful character. The prophet pleads for God to reveal His plan and Himself. As the prophet of God's people and their covenant mediator, Habakkuk was speaking to the people from God and to God from the people. He pleads for God to make the path clear. His final plea is for the God of justice to also be a God of mercy. He petitions the Lord to remember His mercy and remember His covenant. The word "mercy" in the Hebrew is worth noting. It is closely associated with the Hebrew word for "womb" and a powerful description of the depths of the love of God. Like a mother and her child, God pours out mercy. This is who He is, and this is what Habakkuk prays.

The prophet's words point us to Jesus. Habakkuk was the covenant mediator and great prophet, but he pointed to a true and better prophet and covenant mediator. He pointed to Christ, who would be our mediator. As he pleaded for the presence of God in the midst of a season of waiting, we are reminded that we, too, experience in a greater way the presence of God with us as we wait for His return. It is in Christ that our hearts are revived. It is in Christ that God is made known. It is in Christ that God has poured out wrath and mercy. It is in Christ that we have not only received mercy by not receiving the punishment for our sin that we deserved, but it is also in Him that we receive grace. In Him, we not only do not receive what we deserve, but we do receive what we could never deserve. Grace upon grace flows from the cross.

These words should bring us comfort today in whatever season or situation we find ourselves. God is faithful, and He will not deny His own. We do not have to have it all together to come to Him. He simply asks us to come—come in our confusion, come with our questions, come with our struggles, come and be satisfied by Jesus.

IT IS IN CHRIST THAT OUR HEARTS ARE REVIVED.

1 How did the Word of God shift Habakkuk's perspective? Refer to the beginning of Habakkuk to remember where we started.

_____
_____
_____
_____
_____
_____
_____

2 How should God's Word shift our perspective? How should an understanding of God's character move us to worship?

_____
_____
_____
_____
_____
_____
_____

3 Use Habakkuk's prayer structure (revive, reveal, remember) to pray for God's presence in your own situation. Write out your prayer below.

_____
_____
_____
_____
_____
_____
_____
_____

WEEK 3

HE IS THE ONLY STEADFAST ROCK

DAY 3

The Only Everlasting One

HABAKKUK 3:3-7

Our God is a god who comes near. He is the rescue from an unexpected place. He is the radiant Light of the World. He is the everlasting One. As Habakkuk stops to record this psalm, he records for us brilliant imagery to describe God's character to us. We are left with a poetic vision of who God is that should turn our hearts to worship and fill our souls with reverence and awe. Despite the difficulty that surrounds him, Habakkuk is enraptured with a vision of who God is that overflows his heart and pen with adoration.

Habakkuk follows a typical pattern often found in Hebrew worship by recalling the events of the exodus through the beginning of this psalm. The exodus was one of the most pivotal moments of the Old Testament, and it is constantly referenced throughout Scripture as a shining example of God's deliverance. In verse 3, we must stop just two words in to meditate on the truth that God came. He never calls for people to try to work their way to Him, but instead, He comes near to us. Habakkuk looks back to the time of the exodus when God came near at Sinai (referenced here as Mount Paran) to give His people the Law. The text tells us that He comes from Teman. This is south of Edom, though the term is often used to simply refer to the south. Many theologians have also pointed out that this was a place of unexpected salvation. It is a simple reminder to us that God so often works in unexpected ways to accomplish His purposes.

As God comes near, His splendor, majesty, and glory cover the heavens and earth. The language here is nearly identical to Habakkuk's prophecy in Habakkuk 2:14. Habakkuk was not only speaking of events that would shortly occur but also looking forward to a day when all the earth would be filled with God's glory. He looked forward to a day that we look forward to as well.

Verse 4 portrays God as light. This is a common image used to describe the Lord in both the Old and New Testaments. In the context of the Exodus account, we are reminded of the shining glory of the Lord that was too holy and magnificent for Moses to even look upon. 1 Timothy 6:16 refers to God as unapproachable light. This is the splendor of His holiness. And yet our God who is light and in whom is no darkness at all (1 John 1:5) has revealed Himself to us. He has come down. And it is in Jesus that we know the Light of the World (John 8:12). The unapproachable and magnificent light of God approaches us through Jesus.

In the wake of judgment and plagues that remind us of the plagues of Egypt comes the measuring of the earth and a beautiful reminder of God's eternal nature. Habakkuk points us to the mountains. From our finite perspective, mountains seem eternal and immovable. But in contrast to the Lord, the mountains are no more immovable than a speck of dust. He is the only eternal One. He is the only steadfast Rock. And His plan will endure, no matter what may come. His sovereign plan is more eternal than anything our eyes can see.

The enemies of God tremble before Him, but we as His people come boldly and freely before His matchless throne of grace. We are invited near to Him in all of His glory because of what Jesus has done. We are brought near in our brokenness and drawn close in our weakness. We are called out of darkness and into His marvelous light (1 Peter 2:9). We are safe and secure in His eternal embrace, no matter what is crumbling around us. The same God who has come near to us in salvation longs to come near to us each day.

1 What did you learn about the character of God in today's passage?

2 Read 1 Timothy 6:16, 1 John 1:5, John 8:12, and 1 Peter 2:9. How do these verses help you understand what it means that God is light?

1 Timothy 6:16

1 John 1:5

John 8:12

1 Peter 2:9

3 This passage is full of beautiful descriptions of who God is. Which part do you find the most comforting in your own life?

WEEK 3 / DAY 4

THE CROSS IS PROOF THAT WE HAVE
HOPE AND WE ARE NEVER FORSAKEN.

Wait on The Lord

HABAKKUK 3:8-16

Throughout the book of Habakkuk, we are given an intimate glimpse into the heart and mind of Habakkuk and into his relationship with God. This beautiful prayer or psalm of chapter 3 gives us a deeper insight into God's character and of how He works in history. As Habakkuk looks back, we are able to observe what God has done, and we are reminded of how remembering can strengthen our faith as we look forward to the future and the unknown.

In this section of the psalm, Habakkuk shifts tenses. Though the first verses of the chapter spoke of God in the third person as it spoke of His coming, here we see that Habakkuk speaks of the Lord in second person as His presence is imminent. The Lord is portrayed for us as the mighty warrior of His people. We see Him as the one who fights for His people. He is not far off like Habakkuk had initially worried. Instead, He is near, and He is working. Little by little, He is working a plan of rescue and redemption for His children. He is fighting for them. And even though the prophecy that God gave to Habakkuk was one of Judah's coming judgment, we learn that God brings salvation, even through this means.

This prayer of Habakkuk is full of references and similarities to several other prayers in Scripture. The language is shared though not identical with the prayer of Moses in Exodus 15, the prayer of Deborah in Judges 5, and the prayer of David in 2 Samuel 22. In addition, the imagery is consistent with a multitude of psalms. Habakkuk is remembering the Lord's faithfulness to His people in times past as a comfort for His present and future situations. Habakkuk is praying the Word of God back to God. His pleading, his prayer, and his praise are rooted in the Word of God.

Habakkuk continues to reference the exodus, as well as other events where the Lord fought for His people, such as the battle with Gibeon when the Lord made the sun to stand still (Joshua 10:12-14) or the conquering of the waters at the Red Sea, the Jordan, and at Kushon. In remembering and rehearsing God's character and His works and in praying the Word of God, Habakkuk was effectually preaching the gospel to himself. He was reminding himself who God is and how He works. And the words of verse 13 ring out for all of God's people. Our covenant keeping God goes out to fight for His people. He keeps His covenant. He keeps His Word. His plan will not fail.

Verse 16 shifts our attention back to the prophet. The words of this prophecy have not all been easy or optimistic. Judgment was coming because of the people's sin. Habakkuk knew that the same mighty and majestic God who rescues His people would also punish sin. He trembles and quivers as the weight of the prophecy sinks in. The judgment of God is coming, and yet the promise of the Father is that He will be with His own. So with quivering lips and shaking legs, Habakkuk chooses to worship in the waiting. He chooses to trust the One who has been faithful to reveal Himself. Throughout this short book, God has been constant and unchanging. But Habakkuk has been changed by the unchanging One. The prophet who once asked, "How long?" now waits and rejoices in the Lord who is His strength.

Habakkuk felt the weight of the wrath of God that was coming. As the prophet and mediator for the people, the weight of the coming judgment fell heavy on him. But the heaviness that he faced was but a glimpse of the heaviness and weight that rested on the true and better mediator of God's people. In the garden of Gethsemane, Jesus felt the weight of the bitter cup that He was about to drink. He felt the heaviness of the path of suffering that was set before Him (Mark 14:32-42). On the cross, He bore the wrath of God in our place and took upon Himself our sins. He went willingly in our place. He took the wrath of God so that we, as God's children, would never have to. This is the hope of the gospel.

It is this gospel that emboldens us with courage and hope. It is this assurance that allows us to face anything knowing that no matter what life looks like, we are not alone. The cross is proof that we have hope and we are never forsaken. Because of the cross, we can also trust God and wait on Him. With quivering lips and shaking legs, we can trust the goodness of our God. We can persevere through His strength because we know that He is working. He has not left us, and He never will.

HABAKKUK CHOOSES TO WORSHIP IN THE WAITING.

HE CHOOSES TO TRUST THE ONE WHO HAS

BEEN FAITHFUL TO REVEAL HIMSELF.

1 What does this passage teach you about who God is? How can this truth encourage you to trust Him?

2 How does remembering what God has done in the past and knowing the Word of God help us to face what is ahead?

3 Habakkuk prayed the Word of God back to God. This is so helpful for us as we come to the Lord in prayer. Think about what you are facing in your life right now. What passage of Scripture can you pray today?

WEEK 3

WE REJOICE BECAUSE OF WHO HE IS

DAY 5

Even If

HABAKKUK 3:17-19

The final words of Habakkuk are some of the most beautiful words in all of Scripture. They are a reminder of God's gracious sovereignty and our utter dependence on Him. They urge our hearts to contentment and rejoicing. The book started with Habakkuk's despair. He was in a bad spot, and the nation was in a bad spot. He felt like God had forgotten His people, and he was wondering if the Lord even heard his prayers. Throughout the rest of the book, we learned that God did hear his prayers, but we also learned that things were going to get worse before they got better. Perhaps this is what makes the final verses of the book so moving. Instead of being angry that things were not going the way he wanted, Habakkuk had learned to walk by faith and not by sight. And the book of Habakkuk reminds us to do the same. It calls us to stop asking, "What if?" and start saying, "Even if." Even if the worst possible thing happens in our lives, we have the Lord, and in Him, we have all that we need. This is the hope of Habakkuk.

In these final verses, Habakkuk lists for us all the things that could happen, and from his perspective they were things that would happen soon. Most of us don't live in an agrarian culture the way that Habakkuk did, so the things Habakkuk lists may seem odd to us. But from Habakkuk's perspective, he was thinking about total devastation. If there were no figs blossoming and no fruit on the vines, then there was no food. If the crops did not yield and there were no animals to be sold, then there was no income. Habakkuk is thinking about the worst possible scenario. He is thinking about what life would be like if his worst fears came true. And then he realized that even if his worst fears came true, he would have the Lord. And for the people of God, that is more than enough.

"It's all going to be okay." When walking through suffering these words can wound and sting. Because when we are in the trenches of suffering, it doesn't feel like it is all going to be okay. The words sound like a trite catch phrase. But Habakkuk reminds us that for the people of God, it truly is all going to be okay. In fact, it will be far better than okay. Because even when things look bad or like they could not possibly get any worse, the Lord is constant and sure. We have a place to run on the darkest days and in the most mundane seasons. No matter what is ahead of us, He is with us.

So Habakkuk's response to the thought of the coming devastation was confidence and worship. He declares that when things get bad, he will rejoice in the Lord. When things seem like they cannot get any worse, He will find joy in His God. This is the reminder that we need when life is hard. When there is no joy to be found in my situation, there is joy to be found in my God.

And the Lord—He will not leave us. He will be our strength when we are weak. He will be our song when the words will not form and our voices crack through tears. When our feet stumble and we cannot find our way, He will be our solid rock and the firm foundation underneath our wobbling feet.

And whatever suffering we face, we can look to Jesus, who has suffered in our place. We can remember the goodness of the gospel and the truth that He has overcome the greatest enemy of all. We can become like Him in suffering and be molded into His image in our sorrows. And right there in the middle of suffering and struggle and the burdens that weigh on our hearts, we can rejoice. We do not rejoice because of our situations. We do not rejoice because of success or achievements. We do not rejoice because trouble never came. We rejoice because when the fire came, He was with us every step of the way. We rejoice because of who He is.

1 How do these verses encourage you to trust and rejoice in your own life?

_____
_____
_____
_____
_____
_____
_____

2 As you think back on the book of Habakkuk, what have you learned about God from this book?

_____
_____
_____
_____
_____
_____
_____
_____
_____
_____
_____
_____
_____
_____

3 What has been the biggest takeaway from the book of Habakkuk for you?

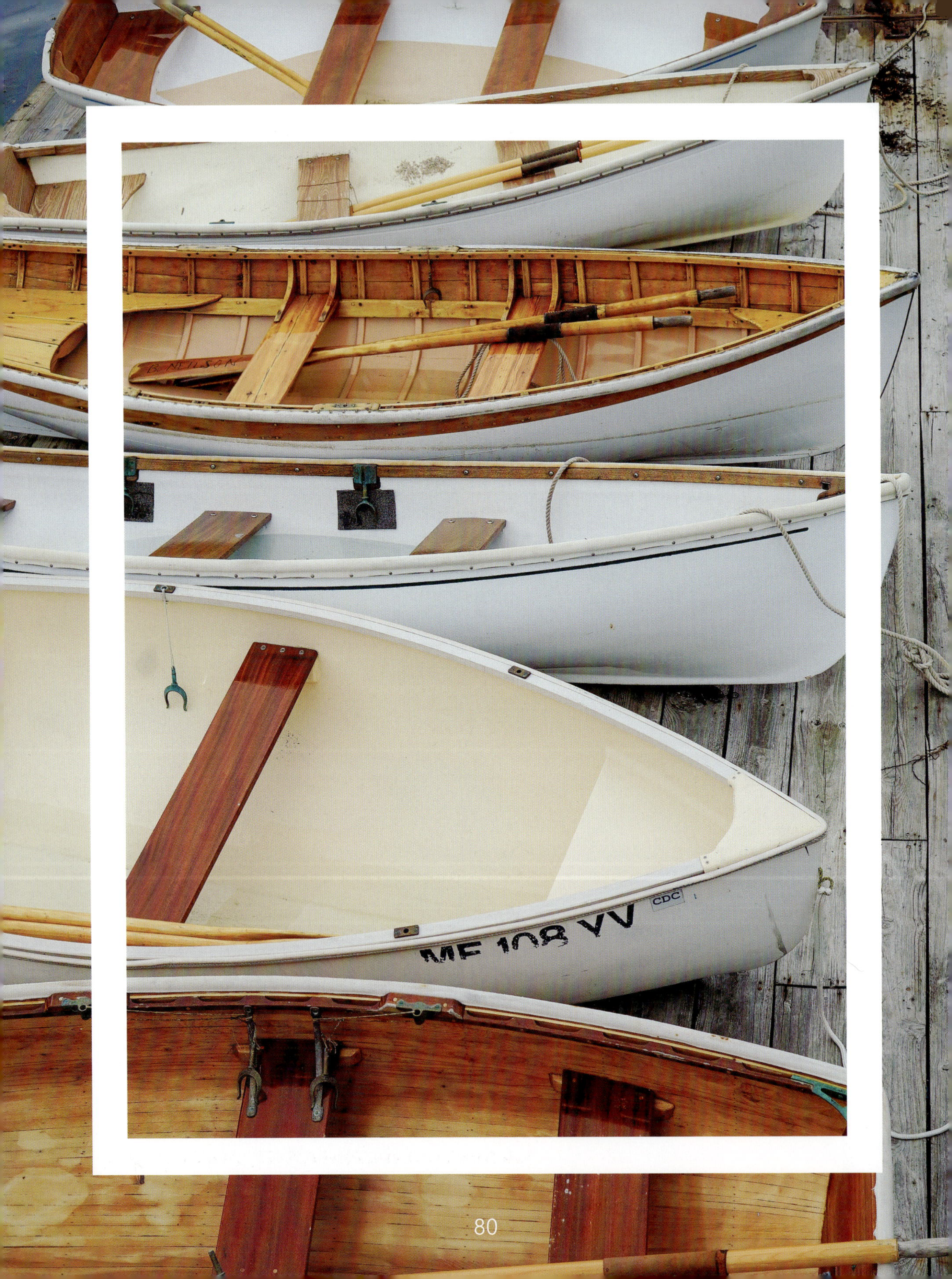
CDC
ME 108 VV

03 MEMORY VERSE

The Lord my Lord is my strength; He makes my feet like those of a deer and enables me to walk on mountain heights! ...

Habakkuk 3:19

Week Three Reflection

Paraphrase the passage from this week.

What did you observe from this week's text about God and His character?

What does this passage reveal about the condition of mankind and yourself?

Habakkuk 2:15 – 3:19

How does this passage point to the gospel?

_____
_____
_____
_____
_____
_____
_____

How should you respond to this passage? What specific action steps can you take this week to apply this passage?

_____
_____
_____
_____
_____
_____
_____

Write a prayer in response to your study of God's Word. Adore God for who He is, confess sins that He revealed in your own life, ask Him to empower you to walk in obedience, and pray for anyone who comes to mind as you study.

_____
_____
_____
_____
_____
_____
_____

HABAKKUK & THE PSALMS

HABAKKUK	PSALM
1:2 *How long, Lord, must I call for help and you do not listen or cry out to you about violence and you do not save?*	4:2 6:3 13:1
1:12 *Are you not from eternity, Lord my God? My Holy One, you will not die. Lord, you appointed them to execute judgment; my Rock, you destined them to punish us.*	18:2 90:2 93:2 103:17
1:13 *Your eyes are too pure to look on evil, and you cannot tolerate wrongdoing. So why do you tolerate those who are treacherous? Why are you silent while one who is wicked swallows up one who is more righteous than himself?*	12:6 19:9
2:1 *I will stand at my guard post and station myself on the lookout tower. I will watch to see what he will say to me and what I should reply about my complaint.*	85:8
2:14 *For the earth will be filled with the knowledge of the Lord's glory, as the water covers the sea.*	33:5 72:19 119:64
2:20 *But the Lord is in his holy temple; let the whole earth be silent in his presence.*	11:4

HABAKKUK	PSALM
3:2 *Lord, I have heard the report about you; Lord, I stand in awe of your deeds. Revive your work in these years; make it known in these years. In your wrath remember mercy!*	44:1 64:9 77:12 143:5
3:3 *God comes from Teman, the Holy One from Mount Paran. Selah His splendor covers the heavens, and the earth is full of his praise.*	48:10 72:19 148:13
3:10 *The mountains see you and shudder; a downpour of water sweeps by. The deep roars with its voice and lifts its waves high.*	77:16
3:12 *You march across the earth with indignation; you trample down the nations in wrath.*	68:30 108:13
3:15 *You tread the sea with your horses, stirring up the vast water.*	77:19
3:18 *yet I will celebrate in the Lord; I will rejoice in the God of my salvation!*	9:14 40:16
3:19 *The Lord my Lord is my strength; he makes my feet like those of a deer and enables me to walk on mountain heights! For the choir director: on stringed instruments.*	18:33

IMAGERY OF GOD'S POWER

IN CHAPTER 3

VS. 3
HIS POWER COMES FROM THE MOUNTAINS,
HIS SPLENDOR COVERS THE HEAVENS

VS. 4
HIS BRILLIANCE IS LIKE LIGHT

VS. 6
HE STANDS AND SHAKES THE EARTH,
HE BREAKS APART MOUNTAINS, HILLS SINK,
HIS WAYS ARE ANCIENT PATHS

VS. 8-9
HE SPLIT THE EARTH WITH RIVERS

VS. 10
MOUNTAINS SHUDDER AT HIS SIGHT,
WATERS ROAR AND LIFT HIGH AT HIS SIGHT

VS. 12
HE MARCHES ACROSS THE EARTH, TRAMPLING NATIONS

VS. 13
HE SAVES HIS PEOPLE, CRUSHING THE WICKED

VS. 15
HE STIRS UP THE SEAS

FLOW OF CONTENT

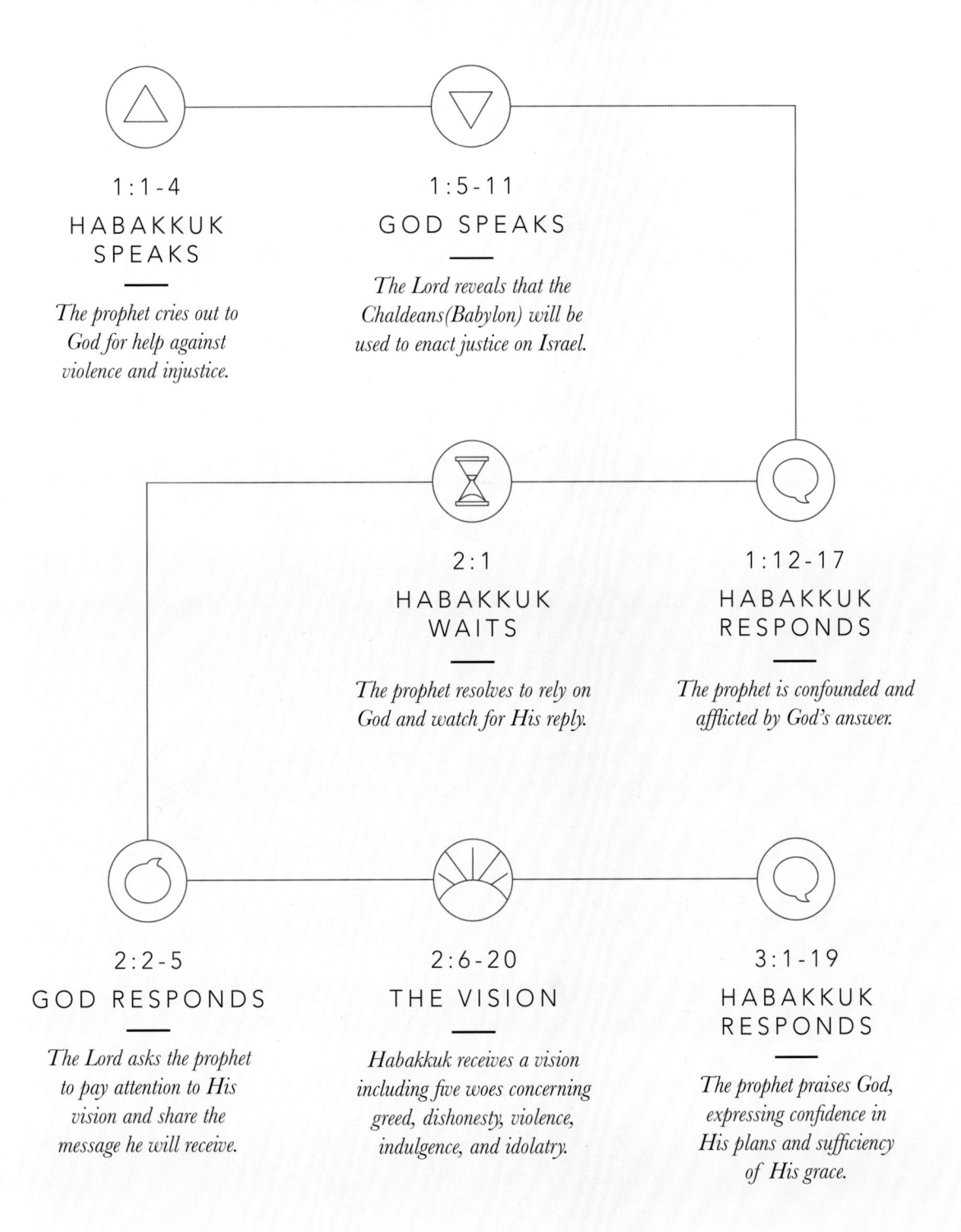

1:1-4
HABAKKUK SPEAKS

The prophet cries out to God for help against violence and injustice.

1:5-11
GOD SPEAKS

The Lord reveals that the Chaldeans(Babylon) will be used to enact justice on Israel.

2:1
HABAKKUK WAITS

The prophet resolves to rely on God and watch for His reply.

1:12-17
HABAKKUK RESPONDS

The prophet is confounded and afflicted by God's answer.

2:2-5
GOD RESPONDS

The Lord asks the prophet to pay attention to His vision and share the message he will receive.

2:6-20
THE VISION

Habakkuk receives a vision including five woes concerning greed, dishonesty, violence, indulgence, and idolatry.

3:1-19
HABAKKUK RESPONDS

The prophet praises God, expressing confidence in His plans and sufficiency of His grace.

The 5 Woes
REASONS FOR DISCIPLINE

①

HABAKKUK 2:6-8

Greed and oppressive financial practices

②

HABAKKUK 2:9-11

Prospering through dishonest means

③

HABAKKUK 2:12-14

The use of violence and slavery to build cities

④

HABAKKUK 2:15-17

Indulgence in drunkenness and lewdness

⑤

HABAKKUK 2:18-20

Practicing idolatry

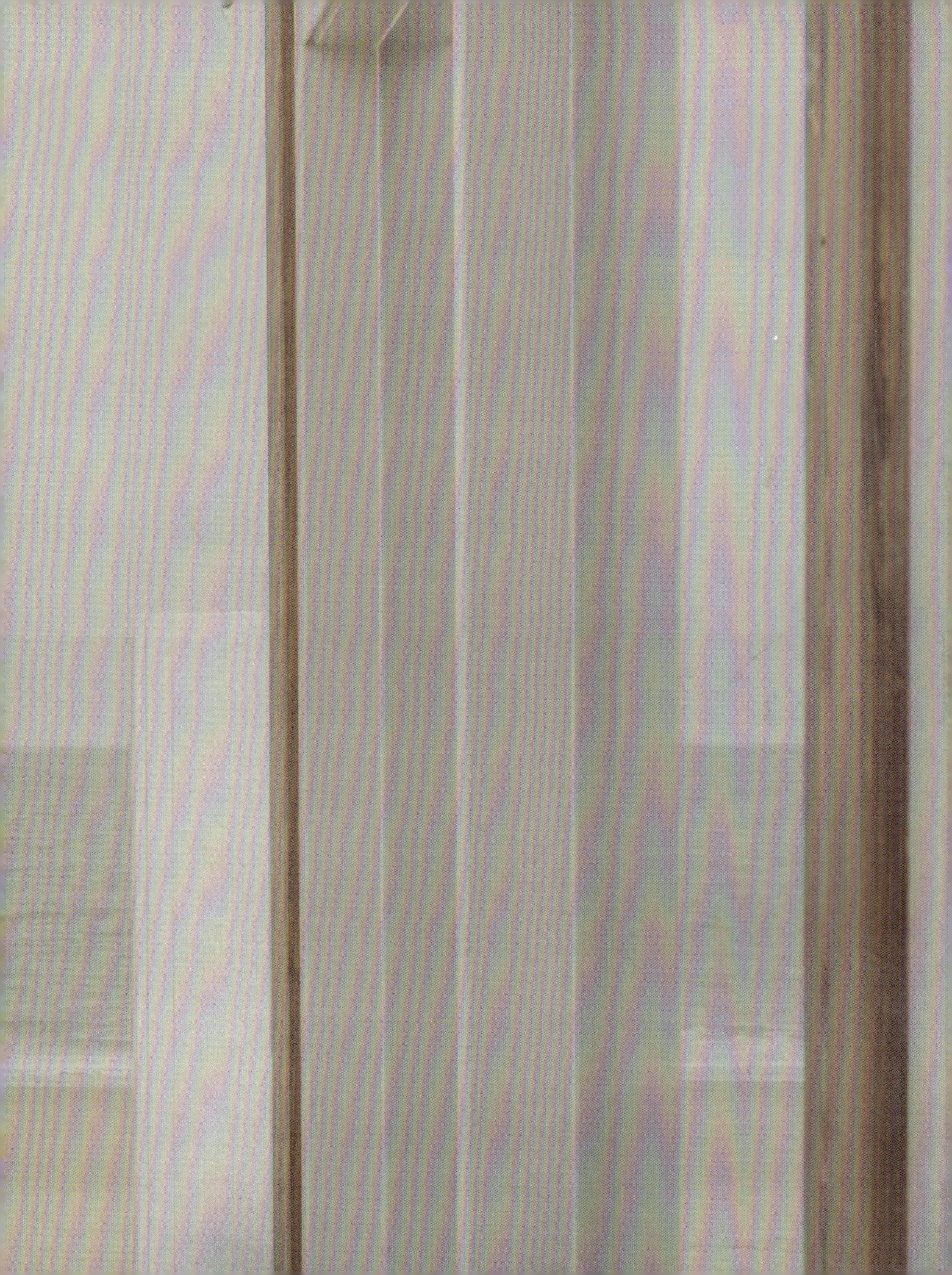

What is the Gospel?

THANK YOU FOR READING AND ENJOYING THIS STUDY WITH US! WE ARE ABUNDANTLY GRATEFUL FOR THE WORD OF GOD, THE INSTRUCTION WE GLEAN FROM IT, AND THE EVER-GROWING UNDERSTANDING IT PROVIDES FOR US OF GOD'S CHARACTER. WE ARE ALSO THANKFUL THAT SCRIPTURE CONTINUALLY POINTS TO ONE THING IN INNUMERABLE WAYS: THE GOSPEL.

We remember our brokenness when we read about the fall of Adam and Eve in the garden of Eden (Genesis 3), where sin entered into a perfect world and maimed it. We remember the necessity that something innocent must die to pay for our sin when we read about the atoning sacrifices in the Old Testament. We read that we have all sinned and fallen short of the glory of God (Romans 3:23) and that the penalty for our brokenness, the wages of our sin, is death (Romans 6:23). We all need grace and mercy, but most importantly, we all need a Savior.

We consider the goodness of God when we realize that He did not plan to leave us in this dire state. We see His promise to buy us back from the clutches of sin and death in Genesis 3:15. And we see that promise accomplished with Jesus Christ on the cross. Jesus Christ knew no sin yet became sin so that we might become righteous through His sacrifice (2 Corinthians 5:21). Jesus was tempted in every way that we are and lived sinlessly. He was reviled yet still yielded Himself for our sake, that we may have life abundant in Him. Jesus lived the perfect life that we could not live and died the death that we deserved.

The gospel is profound yet simple. There are many mysteries in it that we will never understand this side of heaven, but there is still overwhelming weight to its implications in this life. The gospel tells of our sinfulness and God's goodness and a gracious gift that compels a response. We are saved by grace through faith, which means that we rest with faith in the grace that Jesus Christ displayed on the cross (Ephesians 2:8-9). We cannot save ourselves from our brokenness or do any amount of good works to merit God's favor. Still, we can have faith that what Jesus accomplished in His death, burial, and resurrection was more than enough for our salvation and our eternal delight. When we accept God, we are commanded to die to ourselves and our sinful desires and live a life worthy of the calling we have received (Ephesians 4:1). The gospel compels us to be sanctified, and in so doing, we are conformed to the likeness of Christ Himself. This is hope. This is redemption. This is the gospel.

SCRIPTURES TO REFERENCE:

GENESIS 3:15	*I will put hostility between you and the woman, and between your offspring and her offspring. He will strike your head, and you will strike his heel.*
ROMANS 3:23	*For all have sinned and fall short of the glory of God.*
ROMANS 6:23	*For the wages of sin is death, but the gift of God is eternal life in Christ Jesus our Lord.*
2 CORINTHIANS 5:21	*He made the one who did not know sin to be sin for us, so that in him we might become the righteousness of God.*
EPHESIANS 2:8-9	*For you are saved by grace through faith, and this is not from yourselves; it is God's gift — not from works, so that no one can boast.*
EPHESIANS 4:1-3	*Therefore I, the prisoner in the Lord, urge you to walk worthy of the calling you have received, with all humility and gentleness, with patience, bearing with one another in love, making every effort to keep the unity of the Spirit through the bond of peace.*

THANK YOU

for studying God's Word with us

CONNECT WITH US

@THEDAILYGRACECO

@DAILYGRACEPODCAST

CONTACT US

INFO@THEDAILYGRACECO.COM

SHARE

#THEDAILYGRACECO

VISIT US ONLINE

WWW.THEDAILYGRACECO.COM

MORE DAILY GRACE!

THE DAILY GRACE APP

DAILY GRACE PODCAST